MY RAD CAREER

© Copyright 2020 Bill Allen
All rights reserved.

No portion of this book may be reproduced in whole or in part, by any means whatsoever, except for passages excerpted for the purposes of review, without the prior written permission of the publisher.

For information, or to order additional copies, please contact:

Beacon Publishing Group
P.O. Box 41573 Charleston, S.C. 29423
800.817.8480| beaconpublishinggroup.com

Publisher's catalog available by request.

ISBN-13: 978-1-949472-16-5

ISBN-10: 1-949472-16-7

Published in 2020. Printed in the USA.

Second Edition. New York, NY 10001

My RAD Career
BY BILL ALLEN

Dedicated to my beautiful wife, Carol, my inspiration and my heart.

"If you'd like to see more of Bill Allen, don't worry, you will. As long as I have a TV show, Cru Jones has a home. I love you, Cru...If he was hanging from a cliff and I was holding him with one arm and I was holding my girlfriend with the other, and I had enough strength to save them both I would let go of my girlfriend, just so I could make sure that I really had a good grip on Bill."

-Daniel Tosh
on his Comedy Central
TV show, Tosh.O

Bill Allen

FOREWORD

Chances are if you've ever rocked a pair of parachute pants (is that even possible?), had a haircut that would make the lead singer of *A Flock of Seagulls* jealous (check and double check), and wore out at least one Depeche Mode cassette tape (I avoided that trap, thank God), then you might've grown up in the 1980s.

The '80s were distinctive for many reasons, including the Challenger disaster, the Berlin Wall coming down, me moving to Hollywood, and the real beginning of the marriage of extreme sports and the movies.

This was not a Golden Age for Hollywood movies per se, although some of our best filmmakers were at the height of their powers (i.e. Spielberg, Scorsese, Woody Allen, etc.). The decade was mostly known in the film world for blockbuster franchises—*Star Wars, Indiana Jones, Back to the Future,* and *Rocky III* through *XII*. But the action driven films that centered on rapidly growing sports like BMX, snowboarding, skateboarding, etc., became underground cult movies, and helped spur a generation of movie fans to take these sports to the next level. (God, I hate that phrase.)

There were films like *Gleaming the Cube*, *Thrashin'*, *BMX Bandits*, and *Breaking Away* (ok, that last one was '79, quit bustin' my balls) that highlighted these sports in a way that hadn't been exploited by the movie industry in prior decades. These films exposed to the world to a new kind of athlete, with a whole new attitude. With the advent of cable TV and the newest must-have gadget, the VCR, fans could view these films repeatedly, and learn how to do the tricks themselves, from Alaska to Zimbabwe. Tricks that were invented on the Venice Beach boardwalk could be picked up by some kid in Sheffield, England, improved upon, and transmitted back to the U.S. via video osmosis, creating a global movement.

The earliest example of BMX on film was the seminal motocross documentary, *On Any Sunday*, released in the early '70s. The opening shots of the movie of kids in SoCal, racing around on their Stingray bikes in an early incarnation of BMX, created a shockwave across the world that inspired kids to start riding their bikes like motorcycles. I was nine years old when that movie came out, and I sat in a dark theater, mesmerized by these same images, although unaware of the impact they would create.

While these other films are certainly important in the development of extreme sports, and still discussed by those who were influenced by them, there's one extreme sports movie of the era that seems to outshine them all.

As the director Hal Needham (of *Smokey and the Bandit* fame) noted, the film that made the deepest impact of any of his movies was *RAD*, even though it took in a mere fraction of the grosses of his biggest hits and was seen by a much smaller audience.

Why is that?

A young screenwriter named Sam Bernard happened to be walking on the boardwalk one day in Venice Beach, California, when he saw some guys on BMX bikes doing things he never dreamed possible. Tail whips, flips, spins - on BIKES, for God's sake! This was something that needed investigating, and maybe a movie.

After some digging, Sam found out more about the sport. This was the early '80s, and all he had to go on was BMX magazines and the athletes themselves. Before long, he and his partner, Geoffrey Edwards, finished a script about Cru, a hard luck kid and juvenile delinquent, who finds his salvation in BMX.

Soon Sam's friend, producer Robert Levy, became attached to the project, and Robert was able to enlist his old partner, famed action movie stuntman turned director Hal Needham, to climb on board.

Some key elements were added by Hal, including Hell Track, and Cru's character was toned down and made more sympathetic.

Amazingly, *RAD* was a box office flop, probably due to lack of budget for advertising, and panned by film critics, but this didn't stop it from finding an enthusiastic core audience. In fact, according to *Wikipedia,* on the film website *Rotten Tomatoes*, *RAD* received the lowest possible rating of 0% from critics, but an audience rating of 91%, the largest discrepancy between critical and audience reception in their database, from a pool of 10,000 movies.

In my opinion, the reason *RAD* was so well received by audiences and fans who've embraced the movie, was clearly the athletes hired for the film.

Eddie Fiola, Martin Aparijo, R.L. Osborn, Brian Blyther, and Jose Yanez were but a few of the true pioneers of the sport brought in to participate in the filming. These were the top stunt riders in the world, because *THEY INVENTED THE SPORT*.

Hal was able to capture the brilliance of the athletes at the height of their powers, and weave it into a palatable storyline, one we'd seen a thousand times, but these athletes were unique in all the world. To a young bike rider, seeing these stunts performed for the first time on film was a life-altering revelation.

To the film fan who couldn't care less about bicycling, the movie became a metaphor for overcoming obstacles and sticking to one's principles.

This book was written mostly for die-hard *RAD* fans. It was easy to ignore the enthusiasm for the movie until the Internet and social media made it simple for fans to congregate and get in touch with me. It was then I became aware of the impact the film continues to have on generations of people who love it and were deeply affected by it.

Since I was never allowed to own a bike when growing up, I dreamed of being a bike rider with the purity and power of a child who had yet to be told that life is hard.

For fans of *The Secret,* in my mind I connect those early childhood yearnings about bikes to eventually ending up in *RAD* and being so identified with the sport. I had simply spent too much time dreaming about it and thinking about it, even after I got a car and a girl and forgot about my strong desire to be a rider, the dreams waited for the perfect moment to manifest and weave their way into my actual life. But who's to say?

Anyway, I am happy to share with *RAD* fans some of my memories, but I didn't feel I had enough material for a whole book on the subject. However, I do have a lot of stories I felt would not only be enjoyable to the fans of the movie, but movie fans in general, including a chronicle of being an actor in Hollywood during a very dramatic period, and some of the characters I started out with (some who became household names).

Because my overprotective parents would have their way, I never played organized sports in school. I have them to thank that I am able to still walk upright in my fifties. I was the runt of any crowd I was in until I got out of high school (never to take those pesky SATs). I would've been crushed like a wounded June bug on a semi's windshield if I'd dared get on the gridiron with those corn fed, overgrown football players in my school.

However, it did grate on me from time to time as a child that I wasn't allowed to participate, and my good father, Norvin, took notice.

The local Ford dealership where he worked sponsored a Punt, Pass and Kick competition that I would never be a part of, and I would never have won so much as a participation ribbon if I had competed. Dad thought he would ease the pain of me being somewhat of a pariah for not playing football. (This was Dallas in the 1970s, after all - when the idea that Jesus loved the Cowboys more than any other team was born. I reckon he's a Patriots fan now.)

So one day Dad brought home a PPK trophy for me. I suppose he wanted me to display it like I'd earned it, as if the recognition for unearned success is somehow a substitute for the real thing. I appreciated the gesture, but it made me feel even worse, especially because we were both aware he knew better.

So to receive accolades for *RAD* as if I was the actual hero of that movie feels a bit like getting that trophy I didn't earn.

The real heroes were the filmmakers in front of and behind the camera. From the writers, where movies are really born, to Hal Needham, to the supremely talented cast and crew, to the brilliant riders they brought in, all to make ME look like a hero. For a lot of people the illusion worked just as planned and the focus, for right or wrong, falls on me as the "face" of *RAD* to carry on the legacy or ignore the tidal wave it set off.

I do not take that lightly, having been inspired by actors my whole life. It's the reason I choose to do what I do and I find continual strength from storytellers of every discipline, not just actors. It's my wish that someone find inspiration in these pages either for what to do or what definitely NOT to do. So with that, LET'S WALK THIS SUCKER!

CHAPTER ONE

When I was about seven years old I watched my older brother, Sherman, nearly get killed while riding his bike out into the street. He was barreling out of an alleyway on his hulking red cruiser, and a car screeched its tires to avoid hitting him. Unfortunately, my parents watched the same event and my bike riding career was over before it began. They never bought me a bike or let me ride one from then on.

Of course, I found ways to ride my neighbor Alan Roberts' bike and nearly got caught on many occasions. Mom and Dad always promised they would buy me a car when I reached sixteen to compensate, but to someone under ten years old this meant nothing.

The fact that I never had a bike set me apart from the other kids. It was hard to explain, but I felt "special" in a short school bus kind of way. This started a trend of my mother being over-protective, more by setting rules than by providing actual hands-on supervision.

I could never claim to be a bike rider, so I find it ironic that my most acclaimed role as an actor, the one I'm most known for, is the role of a world-class bicyclist.

I got my first acting part at thirteen in the local high school production of *Dandelion Wine*. I was only in junior high at the time; the prospect of joining my big brother's drama department for one of their plays made me feel like I was on Broadway.

The play only lasted two weeks but it gave me the desire to be an actor. The rush of being onstage and the camaraderie was like nothing I'd never experienced—intoxicating.

I grew up in the 1970s in Richardson, Texas, a suburb of Dallas, light years from Hollywood. There wasn't a lot of encouragement from home to become an actor. Although my parents weren't opposed to it, they were too strung out from working too hard to be of any help with my daydreams, and I was too unfocused to pursue it on my own. They were both older when I was born, so they didn't have a lot of extra energy after paying the bills.

Norvin, my dad, was a car salesman even though he had moved to Dallas from Oklahoma to continue his career as a professor of radio and television. Dorothy, my mom, was a full-time nurse. She had a drinking problem that she later conquered and was the main breadwinner. We needed and dreaded her at the same time.

I have a much older half-brother who I met for the first time on his way to Vietnam, and another brother I was very close to who died skiing when I was in my early teens, so things always seemed chaotic.

One could say I fell in with the "wrong" crowd in junior high and high school, but these were my dear friends and several of them remain my friends to this day (at least the ones who didn't drive themselves to an early grave). We wore black T-shirts, listened to the Stones, and were liberal hippies in the middle of the Bible Belt, with a redneck/Texan edge.

I can recall a classmate during class reacting to my liberal attitude.

"Why don't you just shave your head and move to China?" China, that bastion of liberalism. I would've fit right in.

Kirk Harrison was my best friend through junior high and high school. He was the coolest of the "freaks" and tough as nails. He came from a broken home and did not seem to fit in anywhere, especially school. So we bonded over that, I suppose.

Kirk smoked Marlboros by the pack (his first word, his mom claims) and enjoyed being expelled for smoking in the bathroom. It gave him more time to smoke.

We enjoyed getting into trouble together. We were keenly aware that at Richardson High School we felt like we had shackles, not wings.

I spent most of my high school years partying with my friends and cutting class, but I did take Drama. This kept my interest in the performing arts alive even though I never did any high school plays while actually in high school. I kind of felt I was above it all, having been in the aforementioned high school play while still in junior high (what a big shot!), and I didn't like the new Drama teacher, which gave me a good excuse not to participate.

Besides, my big brother, Sherman, went through the professional theater program at SMU and was supposed to be the big actor in the family. I was happy to remain a window washer during the week and a skydiver on the weekends which is when I got my first taste of "big air."

CHAPTER TWO

After my brother graduated from the SMU theatre program, our mother contacted a long-lost cousin who was starting his own film production company in Arlington, only forty minutes from Dallas. Neither of us had ever met Ted, but Sherman was soon hired to help "Pappy" run some acting classes there while Pappy became involved in the preproduction of a movie he'd written about a jockey called *And They're Off*.

As it turns out, Pappy was a huckster who believed he was Ernest Hemingway and Stephen Spielberg rolled into one. He had more than a passing resemblance to the former and the talent of neither. Despite that, somehow he convinced a Texas bank president, Henry Fagan, to invest in his amateurish movie.

I knew nothing of moviemaking at the time but Sherman convinced Pappy to bring me in for the lead role of the jockey - for the storyboards, if nothing else. Ted used me when he shot the movie in a series of still photographs in storyboard form before going into production, and amazingly several months later I found myself in Kentucky getting ready to do my first role in a movie.

However, when I left Dallas for the shoot I didn't even know if I had the job or not - another one of Pappy's mind games.

I called from Kentucky to tell my parents I'd landed the part.

"Bill, we have some terrible news," my father said. My stomach tightened. I could hear defeat in his voice.

"Yeah, what is it?" I asked, sure I didn't want to know.

"Kirk shot himself with a .45 yesterday," he said. "He's dead. Sherman was there when it happened."

My greatest dream and worst nightmare rolled into one twenty-second conversation. Irony has been a theme for me ever since. Of course this news shattered me and I wasn't ready to come home to Dallas, so I missed the funeral. To quote the singer/songwriter Ray Wylie Hubbard, "It was just the first of many bad decisions I was to make for the next 20 years."

I'd known Kirk wrestled with depression from time to time, even overdosing on pills once. Everyone close to him knew that. Even so, Kirk's suicide was just too difficult for me to wrap my mind around.

I was taken to the Lexington P.D. to give a statement that afternoon. It became known Kirk had been playing with handguns for months before turning one on himself.

Bill Allen

A kid in our circle of friends, Neal Bernstein, had a sister who had been killed in a robbery near the same time and Kirk became a "person of interest" upon his death. The actual killer was later found and prosecuted. So the detectives were just doing their job.

CHAPTER THREE

Back in Kentucky, I began training as a jockey with five-time Kentucky Derby Winner, Bill Hartack, for the role that would bring me into the world of movies.

My costars in the movie were Tab Hunter, Oscar nominee Juanita Moore, and Oscar and Tony winner and Renaissance man, José Ferrer. Jose was once the biggest star on Broadway, sometimes with multiple productions he starred in or directed running concurrently. Broadway was even known as "Ferrer Alley" by many for a time. He had a shelf full of Tony awards as well as a successful movie career with a win for the best actor Oscar in *Cyrano De Bergerac*. He was a star of immense talent and impact. At the height of his fame in the fifties he wed the Britney Spears of the day, Rosemary Clooney. They started having kids, seven to be exact. Jose was even interviewed at home by Edward R. Murrow with Rosemary and baby Miguel in tow.

Tab Hunter was an even larger star in his day than Jose, due to the fact that he was a matinee idol in dozens of films. When I worked with him he was still in amazing shape, even in his fifties. Tab was a hulking blonde stud who had been linked with every starlet in Hollywood, effectively concealing the fact that he was gay, a stigma that still grips the movie industry some sixty years after Tab was at his zenith.

It would be hard to not figure out Tab was gay after spending thirty seconds with him. I couldn't care less, more chicks for me I figured. However, it's considered death for a leading man's image so I understood the subterfuge as a necessary evil. By the time we worked together, he'd enjoyed some career resurgence due to starring in *Polyester* for John Waters. He was so kind and welcoming and just seemed happy to be working. It's so cool when people who have so much reason to be jaded remain humble.

Juanita Moore, who played my nanny (more like mammy) was an Academy Award nominee for her role in *Imitation of Life* with Lana Turner. She'd come out of the Actors Studio in the fifties and had studied with some of the greats that came through there including Marlon Brando, an early idol of mine. Juanita was a distinguished actress of some repute who was unfortunately reduced in this film to saying lines that would've been more fitting in a minstrel show. We developed a close bond and I was moved she gave such support to someone so green.

I mention these people in particular, as they were the first "stars" I ever worked with and they showed me how to remain grateful and professional.

Mr. Ferrer convinced Pappy to hire his two sons, Miguel and Raphael, for the film. Miguel played my friend and stable mate while Raphael played my rival.

The lovely and talented Linda Pearl, who played "The Fonz's" girl on *Happy Days,* was also brought out to play my girlfriend but she never ended up doing the role. I remember having dinner with her, toting flowers Pappy's wife had given me and looking like a geek on prom night, AND NO, I NEVER GOT ANY. She was so far out of my league it never crossed my mind. She was years older than I was and suggested I study at The Royal Academy of Dramatic Art in London. (I plan to get right on that.)

The role eventually went to Suzanne Atkinson. I have no idea who she is, and I worked with her for six months.

Miguel and Raphael had a cousin in Cincinnati, ninety minutes away. They convinced George, who was fresh out of business school, to come and be a part of the shoot and he was with us in a matter of hours. Pappy ended up giving him a role as one of my friends at the stable, a minor part. This was his first movie and the first time I'd have billing over George Clooney, but hopefully not the last. George, Miguel, Raphael, and I formed an official clique, and called ourselves the "Danger Boys."

CHAPTER FOUR

George came from a show business family: his father, Nick, was the Regis Philbin of Cincinnati; his aunt, Rosemary Clooney, was a huge pop singer in the fifties; and his uncle was Jose Ferrer, so he'd grown up in and around the spotlight and didn't really know anything else.

It didn't appear that Miguel and Raphael had spent much time with George up until that point, but the shoot became long and arduous (six months playing make-believe in the boonies), so we all got to know one another well. I was easily the greenest in the group and the youngest so was the target of many practical jokes, all well deserved. It was quite the initiation, as this was the most insane film shoot I'd ever see. The delays and overages were egregious, but this being my first rodeo, I didn't know better and assumed all movie shoots were like this.

I grew very close to the actor who played my father, Adam Roarke, who'd made a lot of noise in the '60s as an actor mostly in biker films. He worked with many entertainers who went on to become stars—Peter Fonda, Jack Nicholson, Harry

Dean Stanton, and some of the best directors of the day.

In a move he'd soon regret, Adam ended up turning down a role in *Easy Rider* after his agent expressed concern he'd end up pigeon-holed as a "biker" if he took it. The trend toward "Biker films" was drawing to a close after it had become the modern Western for a time. After that Adam took up drinking as a profession for a change. He was once suspended from The Screen Actors Guild by the guild's then-President, Charlton Heston, for punching out actor Ben Gazzara on set. Ben had gotten in some young actor's face for screwing up and was possibly drunk himself. However it went down, it was enough to set Adam off, which didn't take much at the time.

By the time I worked with Adam, he had stopped drinking and calmed down quite a bit. He ended up moving to Arlington, Texas, after *And They're Off* wrapped because Pappy encouraged him to open a film acting lab. Adam's career was winding down and the prospect of a steady paycheck must've appealed to him.

Adam was from Brooklyn and dripped East Coast Cool (think Anthony Bourdain). He taught me how to move with attitude and how to act for the camera, a technique that's understated compared with stage work.

I spent most of my time off the set with the Danger Boys. We even had a theme song, Steely Dan's "Show Biz Kids."

Bill Allen

"Show biz kids making movies
Of themselves you know they don't
Give a fuck about anybody else."

Though the name "Danger Boys" was tongue-in-cheek, it was actually plenty dangerous to be hanging with this crowd. I remember hearing Francis Ford Coppola once say about filming *Apocalypse Now*, "We were making too much money, doing too many drugs, and we slowly went insane."

This was an adequate description of my time on *And They're Off*. There were often weeks where we were left to our own devices, and occasionally had to put up with the nuisance of actually making a film.

The Danger Boys became pretty infamous among the locals. Our headquarters was located in our hotel, The Lexington Marriott. With a nightclub and a couple of upscale restaurants just downstairs, we didn't have to travel fifty feet to go down the garbage disposal of life. (Beautifully descriptive or just bad writing? You decide.)

One of my favorite episodes with "The Boys" was later termed "Operation Cherrystone." One of the crew members/actors on the set, Tom Myers, became the target of one of the best practical jokes I've ever seen. I'll give credit to Adam Roarke for coming up with this one, but the Danger Boys executed it perfectly.

For a couple of weeks, George pretended to be sick and coughed every time he saw Tom. George went so far as to rub cigarette ashes underneath his eyes to give himself a deathly pallor. We started spreading rumors that George was going into the hospital, probably for the last time.

Everyone on set signed a get well card with heartfelt notes to George. We set a date to have a going away party for him in a few days and during that time we kept up with the charade that George was very, very ill. When the appointed day finally came, we all gathered around the piano bar in the lobby.

The word had spread so there was a big turnout to see what was happening. The mood was somber as everyone sat around the large Plexiglas piano top and the pianist (who we called "Mr. Lapels") played appropriately maudlin tunes. Everyone had cameras, and we were all taking photographs with George. It helped give an air of believability to the event and ensured everyone would be able to capture the climax for posterity. I remember sitting next to Adam and nearly blowing the whole joke with my laughter. I could not contain myself.

The gathering went on for some time with Tom seated by George for the entire evening. At a certain point, George slipped away and put a cherrystone oyster soaked in ketchup in his mouth and returned to the piano beside Tom. Adam stood up and made some excuse to be beside Tom and surreptitiously put his hand on Tom's neck, so he could control his head with his hand.

Adam forced Tom to look at the Plexiglas piano top and George started to cough and wretch with his back raised like a terrified cat. With that, he spit out the oyster (or rather, what appeared to be a bloody piece of his lung) and it skipped across the piano top inches from Tom's face, right into his view.

What happened next all seemed to happen in slow motion. Screams and laughter erupted from the gathered crowd, and flashbulbs like paparazzi run amok shot off rapid-fire. Tom slowly backed away from the bloody lung tissue. As he did this, the color slowly drained from his face à la Wile E. Coyote, and he was oblivious to any activity surrounding him. The laughter came in waves and did not abate for some time. Tom very slowly came to the realization that this was a prank. But the drama of the event took such a toll on him he was off kilter for weeks.

What was I doing during all of this? The sight of Tom looking at this fake bloody lung skipping across the Plexiglas was more than my tiny bladder or I could handle. I pissed my pants like a twelve-year-old girl at a Justin Bieber concert.

By the time I changed and came back downstairs, the laughter was still going strong. For weeks after, I laughed myself awake in the middle of the night at the thought of the prank. Last I heard, George still had possession of the stop-action series of photos that show Tom going into shock.

Good times.

Another of my favorite Danger Boy memories involves a mass vomit party. Sounds like fun, right? On our way to Cincinnati to visit George's family, we decided to stop and eat at a popular restaurant chain in the Midwest—Bob Anderson's.

We had the usual greasy diner-style meal and got back in the car to make the rest of the trip. We had not been on the freeway more than a few minutes when the Bob Anderson biscuits and gravy started "talking" to us. Raphael and George were up front in George's beat up old Monte Carlo, otherwise known as "The Danger Mobile," and I was sitting in the backseat with Miguel.

I'm not sure who got sick first, but Raphael leaned out the passenger window to barf, and we were moving at freeway speed and it had the effect of pissing in the wind. The vomit started to blow back into my face while I sat squirming in the backseat. I soon resembled a Ping-Pong ball in a lotto draw, bouncing in the backseat back and forth knocking up against Miguel who had also started blowing chunks. Soon George couldn't contain himself either and pulled off to the side of the road to heave. Both doors flew open as all four of us bailed out and started spewing all over the side of the road. God only knows what people in the other cars thought was happening as they passed us by but it must have looked horrible, because it was.

From then on we referred to the restaurant as Barf Anderson's.

George took us to his childhood home in Cincinnati and we all got to spend a good amount of time and several meals with his parents, Nick and Nina, and his sister, Adelia. George grew up in a lovely upscale home and had obviously led an idyllic life up to that point. With Jose, Miguel, Raphael, and George's parents, showbiz was a family affair, but they all made me feel a part of their family. Between Nina's carrot cake and their warm hospitality, I cherish these memories.

Nick had a local talk show that ran for years in Cincinnati and ended up marrying Nina, a former Miss Kentucky. So this family seemed to be charmed well before George was squeezed out.

We all went to visit Maysville, Kentucky, where George's Aunt Rosemary grew up and we walked down Rosemary Clooney Street. That didn't seem like much of a big deal to Miguel and Raphael. I mean, doesn't everybody have parents with streets named after them? Adam came along and literally melted in the humidity. Miguel suggested Adam was sweating out drugs he took in the '60s while he searched in vain for a cab in a town of 500.

One of the more precious memories I have was of visiting George's namesake, his Uncle George, the brother of Nick, Rosemary, and Betty. He had managed the sisters when they had a sister act back in Rosemary's early days as a performer, until WWII broke out. He became a bombardier and was apparently never the same. He used to say in a raspy, almost Cajun accent, "I've killed more people with the touch of my thumb than you ever want to look upon."

Of course, this soon became our catchphrase. We imitated him as best we could and it became Danger Boy speak, for lack of a better term, and somehow we thought he was unintentionally the funniest guy we'd ever met.

My time on *And They're Off* wasn't all fun and games though as I took my jockey training very seriously, which meant losing weight and training hard with Bill Hartack. Training with this five-time Kentucky Derby winner/thoroughbred royalty in Lexington at Keeneland, one of the finest tracks and certainly the most historic in the country, was amazing. But it was not without its hazards. I was nearly killed on more than one occasion by horses I was not yet ready to handle. It was easy for one to take off and not be able to stop for anything, and if you weren't fit enough it was not going to end well. Fortunately for me, I had an alert "pony girl" (a man or woman positioned on the track on horseback for runaways) who saved me from falling off a horse at forty miles per hour.

I was soon extremely impressed by jockeys and their abilities. Pound for pound they're among the strongest athletes alive, risking their lives on a daily basis. After seeing what they (along with BMXers) do to make a buck, I kinda laugh at sports played with balls because there's no comparison. (Sorry, sports fans.)

As if that weren't enough, most jockeys have bulimia which is also, sadly, a part of their daily existence. In every jockey's restroom I saw, the final stall was equipped with handlebars on the toilet so the jockeys could throw up to "make weight." They gave it the euphemism, "flipping." It's a gruesome side of the business.

As often happens with actors, the training becomes more involved than the actual filming of the movie. Becoming immersed in the world of horse racing was easy. I was getting world-class training and had the finest horses available to me.

Pappy was confusing to me because I was so green and because he was covering up for major incompetence. As a result, his ego was always out of control and I was mostly terrified of him. He was a sadist of sorts, but at the same time he was responsible for getting me into The Screen Actors Guild and giving me my first job in showbiz, not to mention doing the same for Clooney by hiring him for *his* first film. Pappy was smart enough, however, to bring in an acting coach for me, a man who became my mentor and great friend, Bryan O'Byrne. Bryan was a character actor I instantly recognized from hundreds of TV shows. He was responsible for discovering Nick Nolte and was instrumental in building his career. I felt I was in good hands.

Bryan was still working with his star student Nick Nolte off and on. During a time in the late eighties when I still lived in a fleabag off of Bronson and Sunset Boulevard. You know the corner I lived on well. Practically every shot of the Hollywood sign is taken from this vantage point, and the sign served as both a welcome and a warning that was inescapable every time you walked outside. An actress who lost her career decades before when talkies arrived and killed silent films, Peg Entwistle, jumped to her death off of the top of the letter H on the sign. Seemed tragic and something to shoot for all at the same time.

It was in this atmosphere I thrived, and I consider those salad days among my favorites.

So old Nick was prepping for a musical film called *I'll Do Anything* directed by the great James Brooks. It was maybe not the best idea putting Nick in a musical. For this role, Nick was to play an actor who finds himself on his heels and scraping by.

Nick's own rise to fame was meteoric and he didn't have much of a challenge to get into the business. Being the meticulous actor, he asked Bryan if he knew any struggling actors to check out and help him connect with his role. Of course Bryan volunteered me and I was fine with that. I was a fan of Nick's work and was happy to meet him.

Sure enough, a couple of weeks later I got a knock at my door and standing there was Bryan and the recent recipient of *People Magazine's* "Sexiest Man Alive" cover, looking anything but sexy. Unless you consider looking like you live under a dumpster while it's on fire sexy.

Nick seemed as shocked at the sight of my tiny apartment as I was to see him. It was cool enough for me. It had my James Dean poster I dragged around every time I moved to a new place and my day bed. Books were scattered everywhere. Good ones, too, not just the pop up kind. Nick and Bryan came in and sat on the piece of floor I had cleared for the visit. I had thought of putting up some bookshelves before they came over, but why bother? After all, Nick was looking for an unvarnished view of the unemployed actor's life and here it was in all its puke-stained glory. The dirty walls, sagging ceiling, scary carpet and the sketchy neighborhood were all clearly making Malibu Boy uncomfortable.

Let's face it, he was used to chasing models around the bed on his private jet. Or chasing models around the beach *with* his private jet. You get the idea.

So here was Nick trying to make polite conversation, probably trying to give me his condolences. All the while his demeanor screamed, "GET ME THE FUCK OUT OF HERE AND GET ME A DRINK."

It wasn't long before Malibu Bob was making TV tires to get the hell out of my Hollywood, a place he rarely visited if looks were any clue.

Geez, I didn't expect to exchange numbers with the dude but I was kinda surprised he drove all that way to stay a mere ten to fifteen minutes, tops.

Soon after the production designer came to my apartment to take photos.

So in addition to scaring Nick into bingeing on mouth wash after seeing what fate he narrowly avoided, my little shit hole did contribute to the look of the film.

If you ever see it (I don't think anyone alive ever has) take note of Nick's apartment. It looks eerily like mine. That alone was enough to keep audiences away in droves.

Bryan was only in Kentucky for a month but he, along with Miguel, encouraged me to come to L.A. after we finished filming which I eventually did. Bryan showed me how to break down a script into "moments" that make up the whole. Our contact on the movie was intense if brief. We spoke about the parallels in the script to my life and how to apply that to my performance, a "winner takes all/boy gets girl" kind of story (sound familiar?). The process of breaking down a script and finding what I had in common with the character simply makes for less acting and more "being" when the camera rolls.

I was inhaling the best acting books I could find, but Bryan mostly brushed that aside as "book learnin'" and did his best to help me find the human moments that make a performance.

Bryan tried to get me to treat my new movie friends, the Danger Boys, with disdain because of their outrageous behavior. But to his dismay my reaction was quite the opposite. I aspired to the level of their insanity and did a fairly good job aping their deeds without actually going nearly as far.

I was terrified of the task at hand - starring in a movie while having less on-camera experience than your average caveman. That's probably how I came off, too. Pappy surrounded himself with a seasoned crew, editors, and talent (besides me), but it didn't cover the fact that he clearly did not know what he was doing either, and production delays continued. So the Danger Boys and I continued our antics.

It was obvious we'd become too comfortable at the Marriott when on free taco Tuesday in the downstairs bar, we started to bring our own fresh tortillas and condiments, and then proceeded to eat dozens of tacos apiece.

"This isn't Pete's Taco Bar," yelled the Middle Eastern manager (an anomaly in Lexington, akin to a Jewish guy at a KKK rally) with an accent thick as mud. We thought this was the funniest thing we'd ever heard, I'm not sure why (two gallons of Tequila maybe?), but it gave us the bright idea of hand decorating the tortillas with colored markers. The next week we posted them all over the lobby with "PETE'S TACO BAR THIS WAY" written on each one and an arrow pointing to the bar. I'm sure the manager never got—or maybe I should say, *appreciated*—the joke.

There was an annual pre-Kentucky Derby party thrown by the socialite Anita Madden. At $100.00 per ticket I was determined to make the best of it with my boys—in a rented tux, to boot. This was decadent '80s fashion at its worst. The fact is that I can't remember anything but running into the bathroom stalls to inhale some Bolivian marching powder. It seemed funny at the time, I cringe at the memory now. As the saying goes, "If you can remember it, you weren't really there." Anita's was a standout party because it was the "A" party in town and was attended by politicians, movie stars, and "slut-arazzi." It was one of the last parties I remember where everyone was encouraged to go way too far.

And we did.

The locals treated us like rock stars and were extremely welcoming to the film company, and why not? We spent millions of dollars and provided the townspeople with a reason to contact their doctors at the first sign of a rash.

I was loosely dating a girl back in Texas named Nina and she and my brother, Sherman, came and stayed with me for the last few weeks of the shoot. After all, I'd been there five months already and had lost my best friend. Someone I knew from home had to come witness the insanity I was experiencing. Sherman fit in well with the rest of the drunks I was now calling family, and Nina was happy anywhere - anywhere she could black out after drinking an entire bottle of Wild Turkey, that is. I describe her at the time as Janis Joplin without the talent.

CHAPTER FIVE

I ended up befriending a lot of the jockeys and even met Willie Shoemaker, the most celebrated jockey of all time, on a couple of occasions. Jockeys are cut from the same cloth as a lot of stuntmen I've known. Many are crazy and lucky to find a profession that fuels their need for adrenalin. But jockeys are putting their lives on the line, comparable to matadors. In up to six or seven races a day, these guys put themselves in the middle of a barely controlled stampede of stupid, high-strung, purebred, wild animals being beaten mercilessly by the little men on their backs. It doesn't need to be so dangerous; if folks were interested in finding out whose horse was the fastest, they could run them one at a time. Ever hear of a stopwatch, people?

No, this is a modern-day bloodsport at its best and a cruel and outdated form of entertainment at its worst. That said, there is no more intoxicating world than the racehorse world. It attracts a cross section of society that knows no bounds and the rush you feel of a great horse between your legs, blasting by the rails six inches away at forty miles an hour, must rival that felt by a jet fighter. With the tradition, expense, and athleticism involved, it earns the title "The sport of kings."

But in many ways the jockeys are more abused than the horses. These are full grown men trying to keep their weight at under 110 lbs. – that's including clothes, boots AND saddle. They have little to do on their off time except drink vodka and vomit. Many have found out cocaine is low-cal. Food becomes an endless obsession, and I know for a fact that many of the riders are performing this incredibly difficult and dangerous job while not getting enough calories to even stay conscious in extreme cases. I've wondered often how many horse racing "accidents" have occurred due to low blood sugar.

As for me, I was a skinny kid to start off with at 5'8" and roughly 130 pounds. It was bad enough I didn't know how to act yet was expected to hold my own in scenes with Oscar-nominated and winning actors. I was damned if I wasn't going to at least look the part. So I spent months not eating anything after lunch every day, and quickly got down to 112 pounds.

The Kentucky Derby of 1982 is an event I will never forget. Derby Day at Churchill Downs is something that should be on everyone's bucket list, but few will get to see it as I did. Most of the film company including the Danger Boys (with Big Red in tow), got as dressed up as we could and bought giant foam cowboy hats and mint juleps.

Because I was with the film, I was let into the jockeys' lounge and got to hang out with the jocks that were racing that day. It was a huge field in the Derby, eighteen horses to be exact, and is considered the single most important race in the sport.

So even these hardened pros were nervous, many just biding their time while watching Howard Cosell do coverage of the Derby for *ABC Sports* on the big TV set in the lounge where we were all congregated. Howard announced, "And now for the tragic side of this sport," and a reel of the most horrific racing accidents ever filmed was shown. Looking at the jockeys' faces, I realized they all knew and were likely friends with the riders we were watching being maimed and killed on national TV. It was a horrible reminder of what these guys had to risk as part of their living, and the absolute last thing they needed to see before the big race.

Again, I was given access usually reserved for people who worked at the Derby and got to see the race while actually standing on the track. The sight of eighteen world class racehorses coming straight at you is as impressive as the locomotive sound they produce.

My trainer, Bill Hartack, was feisty, streetwise and smart, and obviously had lived twelve lifetimes in one. He came out of coal mine country in Pennsylvania and clawed his way to the top of a brutal profession.

He'd made and lost more fortunes than I'd had hot meals at that point, so I thought he was pretty cool. He is still tied for the most Derby wins (five), one on Northern Dancer, the most famous stud in racing.

I had no idea if I'd be doing more acting after this, and I was getting trained by one of the sport's icons, Hartack. So getting my jockey's license seemed viable at that point. However, my racing dreams quickly came to an end one day while I was bouncing on a trampoline with Clooney. I did a move that tore the tendons in my ankle so badly you could hear them snap. We were months behind schedule, so delays in shooting were not an option.

As it turns out, the bank president who financed the film, Henry Fagin, had actually embezzled the funds from his own bank. So we ended up going home before completion anyway. So much for my becoming (in Pappy's words) "the next damn Dustin Hoffman." I'd have been lucky to be "the next damn Dustin Diamond." It was back to Texas.

CHAPTER SIX

The next thing I knew, I found myself back in Dallas and I had to deal with my friend Kirk's death for the first time. It seemed like I had outgrown Dallas, yet I stayed another year before I permanently made the move to the left coast. Adam Roarke ended up coming to Dallas to open up what became the Film Actors Lab. We thought of naming it the Film Actors Group, but the acronym didn't work.

Adam, my brother, and Adams' friend from L.A., Dean Marlowe, began what turned out to be a very good film acting school and it's there that I became comfortable working in front of a camera. Too bad that didn't happen *before* I starred in my first movie.

It was also during this time that I landed a role in the Robert Altman film *Streamers* to be shot in Dallas. It was the first time I was on the set with one of my personal heroes. I'd been a serious art house fanatic, and Mr. Altman represented the vanguard of filmmakers that were going against the grain along with Ashby, Nicholson, Rafelson and several others, who were able to make Hollywood films without "going Hollywood." It was a thrill to be in the same room with him.

Streamers was an ensemble piece that was adapted from a play, and I again fell into one of the most rewarding film experiences imaginable. Altman was very relaxed considering something Matthew Modine (one of the stars) told me years later when we worked together again. According to him, Altman was directing the film to pay back some gambling debt and I'm guessing it wasn't the Boy Scouts he owed the money to.

I was lounging around outside of the set one day, an army barracks built inside a soundstage, when I heard my name being shouted and it gave me that old adrenalin rush like I was late for school. I was being summoned by an assistant director to speak to Altman, who was on the set.

For some reason that remains unclear, Bob had me sit beside him as he directed that day. I was dumbstruck at his generosity.

The standout moment for me of that shoot was one that still makes me cringe a bit at the memory. During the production which lasted only three weeks, cast and crew were having a pool tourney at the local sports bar, Dave and Busters, and we were allowed to bring guests. For some reason I thought it a good idea to invite Dean Marlowe from the Actors Lab. Maybe he'd mentioned that he played pool or maybe because he was from L.A. Anyway, it seemed like a good idea at the time, as the drunk said after he was found rolling around nude in a cactus patch.

The day came for the tourney and Dean met me at the sports bar. Coincidentally, Dean bore a striking resemblance to Dean Martin, if someone shoved an air hose up Deano's butt and put it on full blast for five minutes. And the usually dapper Dean showed up looking like he was a homeless person. A camouflage jacket and an unshaven face made him look like the hustler that he later turned out to be. Altman was knocked out of the competition early and retired to have a "jazz cigarette" while Dean cleaned up, one game at a time.

It became evident that he might win and I begged him to throw the game, which he offered to do if I paid him the equivalent of the purse. I was too cheap and stupid or both to take him up on his offer. (I'm no longer too cheap, just the right amount.)

Dean cleaned everyone's clock as I watched in horror. I knew what everyone was going to be thinking, and I was right. He only walked with a couple hundred dollars but to have this interloper come and take everyone's money didn't look good. Altman came back from his smoke break and asked who won the tourney and his money. When he was told it was Dean he simply replied, "Qual supriso" (Italian for, "what a surprise").

I was a big hit the next time I came to set. (Yes, that was sarcasm...)

I had only been studying at the Actors Lab a few months before a hulking Filipino straight out of UT theater school showed up. At first he was a bit too wide-eyed and overly enthusiastic for my laid-back self but he grew immensely as an actor in front of my eyes and became a good friend and a driving force for the Actors Lab, not to mention our softball games.

The world would come to know him a couple of years later as Lou Diamond Phillips, but at the time he was Big Lou. Big Lou had big dreams and one of them was he wanted to portray a musician who had a song so closely associated with the performance you'd think of it every time you heard that song. It was about two years later that Lou was discovered in a nationwide search to play the lead in *La Bamba*. (Cue the *Twilight Zone* theme song about now...)

La Bamba brought Lou to national prominence and I got my first long look at the young and famous. The premiere party was the night Lou became a star, and it was befitting the occasion. It was held at The Palace Theater, a grand old vaudeville house in Hollywood, and the talent onstage included Los Lobos, Brian Setzer, Bo Diddley, and others. I sat next to the legendary blues man Willie Dixon and got to meet some of my idols including John Fogerty and Roy Orbison. It was the party to be at that night, and those who were there will never forget it.

Around this time, I was able to pick up some TV work, and things seemed to be happening in L.A. I got to guest star on some iconic shows including *Family Ties, Hill Street Blues, Hotel,* and Stephen Spielberg's *Amazing Stories*, to mention a few. I got to meet Robert Zemeckis who was casting *Back to the Future*, and I remember sitting around with him goofing on Scientology in the Amblin offices at Warner Brothers. I knew it was a star-making movie. The role eventually went to Eric Stoltz who was fired six weeks into production before Michael J. Fox ended up getting the lead.

So when I shot a guest-starring role on *Family Ties*, Michael was rehearsing *Ties* during the day and shooting the movie at night. It was hard to be jealous because he was very cool to work with, and exceedingly professional while running on zero sleep and lots of Canadian beer. But I somehow managed. I'm not so jealous of him now.

CHAPTER SEVEN

As it so happens, Hal Needham (longtime legendary Hollywood stuntman who already had directed *Smokey and the Bandit* and *Cannonball Run*) was casting his latest movie, a BMX-themed action flick, *RAD*, about this time. He saw my work on *Hill Street Blues* while in pre-production.

As luck would have it, my *Hill Street Blues* episode aired again as he was getting ready to cast *RAD* and he saw it a second time. I guess he had pretty much already decided to use me by the time I auditioned. I only read once for him and the producer, Robert Levy, and writer, Sam Bernard. It was a low-pressure meeting and they actually had me sit on a BMX bike to see how I looked and since I run on the small side (5'8"), I did look like a teenager on it.

That was it for the casting process. It was probably a month later in the fall of '84 that I flew up to Canada for my date with destiny. We shot most of the movie in Cochrane, about a half an hour outside of Calgary.

These are some of the most beautiful parts of North America and the only thing nicer than the countryside was the people. I've been lucky enough to have spent some time since all over Canada and the people are as kind as you'll ever run across. In that way it reminded me of the Southern U.S.

Many of the supporting players were locals and were so excited to be a part of this movie. Their enthusiasm and support is what made the shoot possible, as is often the case. The weather largely cooperated and because Canada is so film friendly, the entire shoot went off without a hitch, finishing early.

I was surrounded by the cream of character actors - Ray Walston, Jack Weston, Talia Shire, Alfie Wise - and the best BMX riders in the world, so I was pretty optimistic about this one. My buddies were played by an L.A. actress, Marta Kober, in the role of Becky, and Jamie Clark, a local and an Olympic hopeful for cross-country skiing, to play Luke.

My arch-nemesis was portrayed by six-time Olympic gold medal gymnast, Bart Conner. Anyone who was around for the 1984 Los Angeles Olympics was mesmerized by the men's gymnastics team led by Conner to a basketful of gold medals. They were so good, in fact, that a couple of the team members got starring roles in movies, one being Bart, the other Kurt Thomas in *Gymkata,* in which he played a guy fighting some bad guys. Whenever there was trouble looming, a bar that he could swing around on would somehow magically appear. Filmmaking on an epic scale. *RAD* was Bart's opportunity, and I promise he did a better job acting on a film set for the first time than I would've done on the parallel bars after a lifetime of practice. He turned out to be the nicest, most enthusiastic guy you'll ever meet, and every bit the all-American hero he seems.

Bart was dealing with chronic injuries that often plague athletes, but his were quite disturbing. He showed up on set barely walking, and no one but Hal was aware of how badly he was injured. Bart was surprised that no one else had been alerted to his predicament.

If you look closely in some scenes in *RAD* when Bart is wearing a tank top, you can see jagged scars on his biceps. I asked Bart once about them and he told me that they happened when his biceps ripped out. I pictured him doing some difficult maneuver on the pommel horse, and his arms exploding. Maybe they did. He was dealing with bad knees at the time, too, so Hal only shot Bart walking from the waist up, since he was having a great deal of difficulty walking. It seemed most weekends, while the rest of the cast and crew were watching Hal's latest stock car race on TV, Bart was back in Oklahoma getting his knees "manipulated," a term I took to understand meant bending and straightening his damaged legs, something akin to bending his knees backwards about 90 degrees.

He was enduring the kind of pain that hardly seemed worth the rewards, by rewards I mean walking, and would drive many to suicide. In spite of that, a nicer guy you'd be hard-pressed to find.

The girl hired sight unseen to play my love interest was the lovely Lori Laughlin. One hires an actress like her to make the audience fall in love with just a glimpse of her – and the strategy worked on me, too. She stunned all who laid eyes on her, and she was great to work with at the same time.

I suppose I had her attention, for a while at least. Lori and I couldn't have been more different, me a Texas redneck/hippie and she a Long Island debutante, a real classy broad. But movie sets are among the most romantic places to meet someone. It's like some sort of high school-era game of footsie takes over.

I'd been around enough to know that she was showing some interest in me without being too obvious. So things seemed to go smoothly, our scenes together went fine. But she was a very private person and I realized this was not going to be easy if we were to strike up a relationship, due to cultural differences, mainly. I never finished high school, and my street smarts hadn't really kicked in yet.

And here's the proof...

There was a local nightclub that had been converted from an old bank, cleverly called "The Bank." It was a hip hang out, and one fateful night Lori and I went there. Among the other things I hadn't learned yet was how to drink and not lose my mind. I had grown fond of the taste of vodka from my jockey days (no calories!) and it gave me the courage to do stupid things.

My RAD Career

It's been so long since, but the story I've told myself over the years goes a little something like this...

We were at "The Bank" and everything was fine and dandy, and the next thing I remember, I was on the dance floor making out with Miss Teen Calgary (legal age I'm sure, gulp) while the chick from *Full House* watched.

Somehow I ended up walking Lori back to the hotel. I was full of myself from all the attention I was receiving, not to mention the Vodka.

I remember waking the next day and, as happens on hangover mornings, the previous night came back in bits and pieces, and not in the right order. I first remembered being incredibly charming on our date and *then* I remembered Lori laughing at me and slamming the door in my face. *Then* I remembered asking her to marry me just before she slammed the door in my face. *Then* I remembered making out with Suzy Rottencrotch in full view of Lori.

I suppose it was purely coincidence that the same night my charm was lost on her altogether, and things were never the same.

I do recall that after this stunt we filmed the scene on the river. You know the one - I throw a rock and splash her and ask her with deep sincerity (everybody now!), *"If I try to qualify, will you be there?"* and we kiss.

Well, the camera was about a mile off so she could've made out with my ear and no one would've been able to tell, and much to my astonishment, she stuck her tongue down my throat. SWEAR TO GOD!!! So I guess she decided to "take a walk on the wild side" with the safety of a crew watching in case I got out of hand.

That was it for the onset romance. Lori was cordial for the rest of the shoot but gave ZERO sign that she was interested in anything I had to offer. Ah well, she doesn't know what she missed. I'm sure it's tearing her up while she gets hot stone massages in her Bel Air mansion that can be seen from the moon with the naked eye. (In case you didn't know, she ended up marrying a fabulously successful Target clothing designer, Mossimo, and having two beautiful kids.)

Not all fans of the movie realize that the film was produced by the actress who played my mother, Talia Shire of *Godfather* and *Rocky* fame, and her husband Jack Schwarzman, an entertainment lawyer who became the head of Lorimar Productions and went on to produce *Being There*, and *Never Say Never Again*. The former is easily one of the best movies of the '70s and the latter marked Sean Connery's return to playing James Bond.

The name of their production company was Taliafilm, and they were producing a couple of other movies during the filming of *RAD* that never came out, including one also shot in Canada titled *Hyper Sapien* starring Keenan Wynn, the gold standard for character actors. I had the chance to talk to Mr. Wynn on more than one occasion.

I was visiting the *Hypersapien* set one day and watched the publicist for Taliafilm, Steve Rubin, receive the drubbing of a lifetime that only folks who've been on way too many movie sets have a way of handing out (think Christian Bale on the *Terminator* set). He innocently asked Keenan, "How are you today?"

I suppose Keenan was reacting to Steve's repeated requests for an interview in the preceding days. Keenan's reply was at full volume, letting Steve know that he was, "TIRED, GODDAMMIT! I'M GODDAMN TIRED!"

Steve got the idea and slinked away. I hadn't seen a real showbiz meltdown from a star before, and it's something I'll never forget.

Poor Steve, oh well. I'll come back to him later.

The *RAD* shoot lasted just six weeks and we came in ahead of schedule. The lack of close-ups and medium shots helps attest to that fact.

During a cast and crew softball game some bad fried chicken made by a famous Colonel was handed out and several of us came down with food poisoning. I suffered my own private Vietnam that night, crawling on the floor like a wounded hyena, conversing with dead relatives, and becoming dangerously dehydrated. I didn't realize I could've called an ambulance but was probably too deranged to figure out the number for the front desk anyway. And besides, I was in Canada and up there the prescription for food poisoning is back bacon and Moosehead beer.

Of course, Hal suffered little ill effect if any. He was the only one in the cast and crew who didn't come down with a cold or flu that everyone else got. He had a special elixir, made in oak barrels in Scotland that he administered to himself nightly, that had an amazingly restorative effect.

The first time I was able to have a drink with Hal was the night before the first day of shooting. He asked but one thing for the duration of the shoot. It was a simple request for me - to be on time. He described the shoots for the *Cannonball Run* movies as prime examples of why being on time is so important.

They had twenty-five star trailers in the desert and attempting to get Sinatra, Dean Martin, Sammy Davis, Burt Reynolds, and the rest on set at the same time was a major nightmare.

He told me one of his least favorite people to work with was Shirley MacLaine.

Few will remember that Shirley's first movie after her Oscar-winning turn in *Terms of Endearment* was the probably more watchable *Cannonball Run II*. She turned out to be such a pain, that one morning Hal came to her and said that she would be in charge of filming that day and let her set up an elaborate tracking shot that took the whole morning to prepare. Behind her back he went to the cameraman and told him that if there were any film in his camera he'd be fired. Shirley got to feel like a big shot, and Hal got to sit back and laugh his ass off. Sometimes an enormously expensive practical joke is worth the effort.

He let me in on another goof he played, this time on a judge who had essentially sentenced Hal to community service. Seems ol' Hal forgot about the handgun he had tucked away in his briefcase while going through security at LAX. Knowing Hal, this was entirely plausible.

So the judge, in lieu of a prison sentence, made Hal agree to make some sort of PSA or traffic film. He was able to convince the judge to play a judge in this film, and then cast a large breasted woman to be in the scene with him. Again Hal got to sit back and laugh as the judge blew take after take. Pure Hal.

The first day of filming *RAD*, Hal's little grey-haired mother came to the set and led a prayer of protection for everyone involved, a ritual I later learned from Hal's biography she did on every film he directed.

These were people who came up from dire poverty in Arkansas – we're talking Dust Bowl, no shoes or winter coat poor—and she got to watch her son be one of the biggest successes in Hollywood history. I was unable to appreciate the scope of his journey then, but we often don't in times like that.

Hal made a party of what are called "dailies." Also known as "rushes," it's when the previous day's footage comes back from the lab to be viewed the next day by the director and crew and whoever else happens to show up. With the advent of digital cameras, it's a ritual that's quickly dying.

In this case, the pro riders were invited to watch, adding to the circus atmosphere. Along with the rest of the cast and crew, and as much to drink as you dared, these turned out to be quite an event. Added to the mix was watching the best examples to date of BMX stunts, filmed by the best action filmmakers. It was breathtaking. I was the only actor that seemed to go. Most don't like watching themselves during a film's production.

I should mention that John Schwartzman (son of Jack and step-son of Talia, the producers), and Robert Brinkman, now two top directors of photography, shot the behind the scenes footage that has never surfaced to this day. I'm sure it's priceless. John is also responsible for filming the opening and closing credits for *RAD*.

The worst injury I can recall during the shoot was suffered by Rick Moliterno (now a successful bike manufacturer, Standard Bykes), when he broke his ankle on the series of foot high berms that caused a bit of trouble, as it was hard to get enough air to get over them. After he was injured, Hal threw him a line in the movie (the scene when I signed his cast), a classy move, I thought.

My little sister, portrayed by Laura Jacoby, was one of those showbiz kids that seemed to be born in a trunk. A seasoned actress by the time we worked together, she always held her own and seemed incredibly comfortable and relaxed (the key to good acting) every time she was on the set.

I was joined by her on weekend bike rides as well as an eight-year-old Jason Schwartzman (Jack and Talia's other son), who you likely don't need me to tell you has gone on to have an awesome career as an actor and musician.

Jack Weston (Duke Best), Ray Walston (Burton Timmer), and Talia Shire (Mother), were the cream of the crop as far as their resumes and flat-out acting chops. I had been a fan of Jack Weston since childhood. He was one of those actors who was always interesting to watch, no matter the quality of the material. I particularly loved an episode of *The Twilight Zone* called "Nightmare on Maple Avenue," in which he put in a standout performance. I was impressed that after *RAD* Jack went straight into filming a movie with Dustin Hoffman and Warren Beatty, *Ishtar*. I figured he really knew what leading actors to support (see how I can make anything about me?). Jack had a secret method of achieving his spot-on acting ability. I know, 'cause he offered me some from a flask he kept in his suit pocket. I never question how a good actor works, and this method seemed to work for him.

I didn't have any scenes with Ray Walston but he represented the townspeople in a dignified fashion and played the part perfectly. For filmmakers who might be reading this: getting the very best actors to do even the most thankless of roles such as Ray had will often pay off in ways no one can predict. He wasn't even at the end of his career at that point, as he went on to work on *Picket Fences* for several seasons, a hit TV show in the '90s. He was hired for *RAD* thanks to his performance in *Fast Times at Ridgemont High,* a very popular film at the time with kids.

Talia Shire was someone I was intimidated by, with good reason. Number one was that she was my boss, being an executive producer on the movie. But more than that was her track record as an actress. As I mentioned already, she starred in two of the most successful movie franchises in history, the *Godfather* and *Rocky* movies. Even more intimidating was what her family (the Coppolas) represented then and now—some of the best entertainment ever produced in Hollywood and the closest thing we currently have to a show business dynasty.

However, my visceral reaction to "Tally" was something that worked for the performances. It's always easier to use a strong personal reaction or attraction to a fellow actor rather than have to manufacture an attitude. I had little interaction with her off the set or at dailies, something I should have maybe rethought at the time. It was easier to just not initiate contact as we had our own lives and she was surrounded by family.

Probably the most unsung hero of the *RAD* shoot was Jose Yanez. He invented the backflip and at the time was the only person in the world who could do it.

Consider that for a moment... Twelve people have walked on the moon, and that's twelve times more people than had done a backflip when Jose first did one. But only Neil Armstrong can claim to be the first man on the moon, and for BMX fans,

My RAD Career

Jose holds that distinction. He was that kind of pioneer, brought on to do that trick and that trick alone. I believe that one decision made the movie.

To watch Jose do it actually felt like watching the moon landing and it was treated with similar gravitas. Each time Jose performed the trick complete silence would be called for on set. He would get on his knees to pray and everyone would join in. These were tense moments.

Backflips are now routine in competition, but not then. This was a big deal. It's still one of the most dangerous moves in sports. The scene where Christian points out to Cru that he "over rotated" is cut together from a botched attempt by Jose and again, Hal just had me get cut into the scene landing on my back and there you have that reality lent to the scene. Catching happy accidents is what directors hope for every day. But Hal made an art of setting them up and weaving them into a sequence.

I didn't spend a lot of time with the riders off the set either. They were mostly younger than me and Eddie Fiola was competing on weekends when not filming. That's the reason that Martin Aparijo did the double work for me in the "Bicycle Boogie" sequence. Eddie had a competition out of town that week and yes, he did win it. But it knocked him out of the chance to be featured in the most iconic scene in the movie.

Eddie told me a story I thought was a good illustration of what it takes to do what these guys do. Ed lost his father at an early age and instead of turning to drugs he turned to bikes, and as a result broke too many bones to keep track of over the years which made his poor mother think he had some sort of death wish due to the loss of his father. But Ed said it was only about learning to ride his bike and do the tricks he became famous for.

The centerpiece of the film and for most, the sequence held in highest regard, is Hell Track. This was Hal's idea and he pulled it off amazingly well. In the original script the race was a regulation BMX race but that wouldn't have been nearly as exciting as what became Hell Track.

Riders were consulted in the construction and were enthusiastic about it - until it was built, that is. Daunting wouldn't describe how it looked in real life. Terrifying would be more appropriate.

Along with the main stunt riders, we had at least two-dozen riders come in for the filming of the Hell Track scenes.

The most difficult hurdle in Hell Track turned out to be the first one, the starting wall that began the race. I can tell you from standing on the starting gate (more than twenty feet up), it looked to be a sheer drop. At first there was no one willing to take the chance and be the first one to pedal off of it—and these were not guys who were used to ever chickening out.

I only recently found out that my stunt rider for the sequence, fifteen-year-old Beatle Rosecrans, was more afraid of the repercussions from telling his old man he refused to ride the wall than he was of falling so he was the first to go for it. However, he began in baby steps, so to speak. He set up a ladder next to the wall and dragged his bike up to start, first from halfway, and increasing in height until he actually did it from the top. I'm not sure how he worked the transition from the ladder, but the other riders were compelled to do it from the top once Beatle did it.

As the filming day for Hell Track approached, a soaking rain came and flooded the set. Someone had the bright idea of hiring a helicopter to hover over it like a giant blow dryer, and they did. It saved the day and the track was dry in a few hours. There was plenty of excitement filming Hell Track, as this was an unproven track and the probability for error was high. In fact Hal depended on it. He cleverly set up half a dozen cameras to capture the action and waited for "accidents" to happen - and happen they did. (Anyone remember the Kix Cereal Bowl crash?) The crashes were edited into the final cut and it played beautifully.

Another actual crash that made it into the film was when Eddie fell, going off his bike on the trail in the qualifying race. This was unplanned as was when another rider smashed into Ed as he tried to get back up, putting a pedal right into his temple. This gave these scenes a sense of reality and drama and is in part why the film is still watched over and over.

The other scene that seems to get the most attention is one I've already mentioned: the "Bicycle Boogie" scene.

Eddie went out of town that week so my double was Martin, and for Lori it was Pat Romano in a wig again. Poor Pat. (Maybe that's why he didn't come to the 25th anniversary celebration in Canada. He was in a bad wig most of the time he was on screen so who can blame him?)

As I said before, I was barely conscious during the filming of that sequence due to some bad chicken. So when I mouth the words, "Who me?" to Lori in the gym I could barely even sit on that bike.

Most of the shots are of well-disguised stuntmen doing the riding or Lori and me on bikes fixed to dollies and filmed so you can't see them. The first shot in that sequence where a dolly was used is when Lori waves me into the gym and then rides off. When she takes off, the bike lurches and (as Eddie observed) she moves like a vampire hanging on for dear life. Check it out.

But when I suddenly appear (with friggin' sequins in my pants!!), that's when you know that I've been hit with an '80s stick, not to mention the twins with their matching Buck Rogers jumpsuits, or Foxy in the purple catsuit.

There has to be some mention of the dance sequence with Bart and the crew. Remember, Bart could barely walk so there was a lot of clever double work with him. The choreography is hysterical and yet somehow watchable on repeated viewings. (It's probably the cat suit...) And then Bart gets to utter what may be my favorite line in the movie (to Lori), "You could've at least waited until I was finished dancing." Profound words, indeed!

Obviously my favorite scenes are the ones I'm part of, and the supporting cast made it a joyful experience. Alphie Wise, Jack Weston's sidekick, was a particular favorite for his stories about being a swinging bachelor and hanging with Burt Reynolds back in the day and being the "Frito Bandito" (remember that racial stereotype, kids?) for Mexican print ads.

I was only hurt once during filming. It was between takes and I was messing around on my bike. I was speeding along a side street and accidentally hit the front brake instead of the rear ('cause I was THAT good!), and it only took a millisecond for me to realize my mistake, 'cause I nearly died. I smashed my head pretty good on the pavement, and it drove home the message, "WEAR THOSE HELMETS!!"

I spent more time on the weekends with the stunt guys than my cast mates, as they seemed to have more fun than the actors. I don't remember getting into too much trouble during the shoot (even though these guys really should have been called Danger Boys), but that came later during promotion of the movie.

Another scene that's talked about, if only because of the name, is the infamous "ass sliding scene."

Unfortunately, it wasn't nearly as dirty as it sounds, but if you're going to go ass slide with anyone, it might as well be with a twenty-three-year-old Lori Laughlin. Launching into that water might look fun but I assure you, it was melted snow and it was COLD!

We were in wetsuits, but that only helps if the water has some time to warm up to your skin temperature. Luckily, we were in just long enough to only THINK we were going to die of hyperthermia. Hal actually told the stuntman who tried it before us, Martin, to come out of the water looking like it was no big deal, and to come out smiling so as not to scare the crap out of Lori and me. Hal shot it from two angles with two cameras simultaneously, so it looks like we did it twice. He was concerned we might not do it again if asked for a second take.

I can tell you I would have slept in that river if he'd wanted me to. The desire to get a movie done at any cost can take over a set and have dire consequences. I was to find this out years later.

CHAPTER EIGHT

The promotional tour was a highlight for me and it was as unusual as the movie's subject. It started with a limo picking me up in front of my seedy Hollywood apartment, not an indicator of things to come.

The tour consisted of a custom-painted van pulling a quarter pipe and carrying the promoter, Bob Destry, our riders, Flyin' Brian Blyther and Rich Sigur, and myself. We hit several cities back East and ended up in NYC.

The tour mostly consisted of local TV covering us at small strip malls and bike stores, but there was always a children's hospital on the itinerary, visits that haunt me to this day. Stopping at these hospitals was supposed to be good publicity I suppose, although it generated none, and that's probably a good thing. Helping kids carries its own reward.

To look into the eyes of a child who was not going to make it and was fully aware of the fact, was profoundly sad. Most were unimpressed by a glossy photo signed by someone they'd never heard of. Some were cheered up by the tricks, performed in mostly makeshift areas, but not cheered enough, and it made us grateful to stop at places other than hospitals.

All in all, this was a very exciting time as the box office story was yet to be told and I had an easy job of being the spokesperson for the film while the other guys risked their necks on the quarter pipe. It wasn't a bad way to meet chicks, either, and I always seemed to go for the ones that presented a challenge. Pam from Philly was no different. With wild black ringlets and as cute as a button, she wasn't impressed with the trappings of Hollywood, and that was pretty cool in my book. She took me to a Grateful Dead concert, which was also pretty cool. Afterward I held her hand as she cried, because her Camaro had been broken into while we'd been at the show.

So when she said she'd meet me in NYC at the end of the tour I thought it was a sure thing (if you get my drift), up until she called and said she was coming with her sister. *HER SISTER*. There goes the party, or so I imagined.

I did the natural thing and had Bob lie to her that I had to leave the tour suddenly to take care of some business back in L.A. She saw right through his stupid story (they had phones back then too, I could've called) and she told him so. I felt lousy about making a liar out of Bob and giving this girl the runaround. I called to apologize, and we both agreed I was an a-hole and left it at that.

I felt horrible. But that wasn't the last mistake I was to make on that tour.

My RAD Career

I found out while we were still on the road that the L.A. premier was about to come up and I asked the publicist, Steve, if I could go. He delivered the tickets and on the way to the airport (in a limo, mind you) I saw that they were flying me COACH (*GASP!*) and I made up an excuse and went back to the tour. This was a "BOZO BIG TOP NO-NO!"

What I failed to realize is that going to premieres is an actor's duty come hell or high water and this was no different, even if it was my idea to go in the first place. My absence did not go unnoticed by the powers that be and I would find out soon that you can be fired even after you finish a job.

So I completed the tour and landed at the airport in L.A. and waiting for me was... nothing. No limo, no town car, no cab, not even a rickshaw. I think the picture was getting clearer.

And who can forget when weeks later I was at my apartment on Bronson and Sunset with my acting coach, Bryan, and we were watching the taping of the annual Hollywood Christmas parade while the stars were being let out of the fancy floats and decorated cars right under my bedroom window?

What I didn't know was there was a convertible with the cast of *RAD* (Talia, Bart, sans ME) and stunt riders carrying a banner announcing the release of the movie. I found out later that Steve Rubin, our intrepid publicist, was also in the parade car. Did you catch that? The publicist was in the parade, *but not the star*. Okay, okay! I get it already.

There's a great picture of me taken by Bryan - I'm leaning out the window with a forlorn look on my face watching the rest of the cast being dropped off right in front of my apartment. It's kinda like the famous Wright brothers picture in reverse. While they're watching their dreams take off, I'm watching mine crash.

So when the movie came out and did not fare well at the box office, it seemed that was that. No sequel, no cover of *People* magazine—I could always get my table at Denny's back.

CHAPTER NINE

Due to some foolhardy business decisions on my part, my acting career was better before *RAD* than after. *RAD* didn't make enough waves at the box office to make much of a difference and I put the experience on the shelf. It was painful that all that work seemed to not pay off and I was right back where I started, only this time without a good agent. So I decided to go back to acting class, get back to the basics and focus on the work - always a good thing for an artist trying to find their way.

I was a pupil of Bryan O'Byrne again. He started an acting class held at the big Methodist church at the corner of Highland and Franklin in Hollywood. My brother moved out to L.A. at the time, and I was establishing a supportive group of actors around me. I will forever cherish the times we had as young artists pushing one another to get THE WORK (and THE GIRLS!!).

Bryan went to a play one of his students, Janet, was doing in a shoebox theater on Santa Monica Boulevard in Hollywood. This would change things for me drastically.

He talked about one actor he was particularly impressed by, George Davis. Remember, Bryan was the first guy to encourage Nick Nolte to take up acting. He had a real eye for talent.

Soon after that, one of the leads of the play dropped out and Janet said I should come down and meet the director to possibly step in and take over the young lead role. Someone already had but he was a good fifteen years too old for the part, not to mention balding, not good for someone playing a teenager.

The play, *When Ya Coming Back, Red Ryder?*, was one I was familiar with and I went to see the matinee the next day. It's a modern retelling of *The Petrified Forest*, a famous play and movie from the forties and a good showcase for the two leads. The other lead role was portrayed by the actor Bryan was extolling the virtues of. He had good reason.

George Davis, an ex-jock from Oklahoma University and brother to OU quarterback legend, Steve Davis (who – no kidding, I found out while writing this, died while piloting a jet!), was a Southern fried Brando. George was clearly the black sheep of the family for going into showbiz, but at the same time a very hard drinking product of his hometown of Sallisaw, Oklahoma. Anyway, you couldn't take your eyes off of him onstage, and I was anxious to work with him.

At one point he'd made the decision to move back to Oklahoma from L.A. to marry his high school sweetheart, Bobbie. He'd been offered a role on a new show called *The Dukes of Hazzard* but had already told everyone he was leaving. That was the closest George came to making it. Prior to that, he was so broke he once shoplifted some ham but suffered an attack of conscience so went back and traded it for some cheaper bologna. That's the kind of guy he was. Eventually he moved back to L.A. and started a theater company.

A meeting was set up behind his back with the director, John Lee Hancock, because George (who was also the producer of the show) was friends with the aforementioned too old and balding last minute replacement.

The first thing John told me was that he planned to ride George's coattails into a glorious future in show business. And since George was so good and had such confidence in John as a writer and director, I had no problem believing John. I ended up doing the role and forged a deep relationship with both George and John. We ended up founding a theater company together, Legal Aliens, and John started writing original works for us.

At the time, John was a starving writer from Texas who'd walked away from the opportunity to become a full partner in a prestigious law firm back home. He was destined to come out here and become a studio writer and later director (writing and/or directing *The Blind Side*, *The Rookie*, and *Saving Mr. Banks*, among others) and he seemed to know it. At least he knew he was talented and he knew what he wanted, and he was the hardest working person I'd met at that point, a recipe for success.

But at the time we were still feeling around in the dark for what we'd hoped would be there – some of us found it, some didn't, and others died trying.

I was getting restless in Bryan's class so I started studying at The Beverly Hills Playhouse at the prodding of my old friend, Miguel Ferrer, who taught there sometimes. He was closely associated with The Playhouse, founded by famed acting coach and Scientologist, Milton Katselas.

Scientology was something I'd never heard of at the time and came to abhor, but it was not part of the curriculum and I wasn't studying with Milton anyway.

Bill Howie was my teacher there at first, and it was in his class that I ran into Clooney again, who was one of the students along with his buddy, Grant Heslov (who was by his side at the 2012 Oscars, accepting their golden statues for producing *Argo*).

It wasn't until I started studying with Milton's tall and pretty ex-wife, Lynette, that I started doing work that I could be semi-proud of, but it was required considering some of the people in that class were off the charts talented, and now the world knows it. Adam Sandler, Paula Poundstone, Jane Leeves, Faith Ford, and Jason Gould (son of Barbra Streisand and Elliott Gould), were just a few, and were standouts before they so much as opened their mouths.

My RAD Career

I actually got to meet Jason's famous mom once. Lynette decided we should rent out this showcase venue on the Sunset strip called the Tiffany Theater and put up some scenes we'd been working on for "industry" people (meaning our agents and families).

The showcase included some of the best players in her class including Jane Leeves, Faith Ford, Jason Gould, my roommate John Nelson (son of David Nelson of *Ozzie and Harriet* fame), and me. I'm not sure how I made the list. Lynette MUST'VE secretly desired me. Yeah, sure, that's the ticket.

Jason and I decided to be clever and do a piece that's virtually NEVER done, live or not, due to the estate of the author never sanctioning any enactment of his works. That piece was from *The Catcher in the Rye,* the most famous novel of the last seventy years, revered by fans like *The Bible* to Christians. Since this was basically a private, non-profit performance, we decided we'd be safe to do it.

Well, it was J.D. Salinger's vehement desire that his work not be reinterpreted and ol' Jerry got his revenge that night.

This was a fancy shmancy theater on the Sunset strip, and we were live with tested scenes that we'd buffed to a glossy sheen in front of a hometown crowd. What could possibly go wrong?

For *Catcher* fans, we were doing the scene that takes place in the bar when Holden grills his sophisticated friend about his love life. It's a very funny scene when done correctly, but a very lame scene when done incorrectly. Bet you can't guess which way it went that night.

Jason played Holden, and I tried to pull off his sophisticated friend as best I could. The sophisticated bit didn't last long. We got onstage and launched into the scene and tried to breathe life into it. I said a line of dialogue and the next thing I knew I suddenly saw the look in Jason's eyes that any theater actor will recognize, the old "deer in the headlights/I forgot my line" look, his eyes pleading for a freaking lifeline, like this was an episode of *Who Wants To Be A Millionaire?* Crap. If Holden were a real guy he'd have called me a phony bastard for even attempting to do this, and now I had the fun job of IMPROVISING J.D. FREAKING SALINGER in front of a packed house.

So the timing of the scene had already gone out the window, the energy had gone through the floor, and it was up to me to fix it 'cause Jason was clearly not gonna help. Worse, it looked like *I* was the one who'd dropped the ball because Jason was staring me down (as was the audience!), waiting for me to say something funny. Only the cast backstage knew what really happened.

Somehow I figured out something semi-appropriate to say and spat it out but not soon enough to save the already brief scene, one that's a hit or a miss kind of scene already, and we clearly whiffed. Ooofa.

So after the showcase the lobby was full of well-wishers for all the people who'd had a successful night. I was not one of those.

However, I saw Jason in the corner talking to Babs, and not unlike Oprah when she writes her "This I know for sure" ramble every month in her magazine, I knew Jason would never introduce me to his mom in a billion years even If I begged him, phony bastard, and which I'd never do because I'm not a fan of hers anyway. But I figured I'd cross the room to get a closer look.

I walked up to them and made up some story about someone wanting to talk to Jason and now he HAD to introduce us, me not realizing she was sure to NOT be raving about my performance (can you tell I'm still pissed?).

"Hey Bill, this is my Mom."

Of course the phony bastard wouldn't say her name. He probably didn't do that 'til he was forty.

I shook her hand as she said hello and for the second time of the night she looked at me dumbstruck waiting for me to say something, and I got nothing.

With zero preparation or debriefing, I was suddenly staring into a face as famous as the Queen of England and I said with zero aplomb, "I've heard a lot about you," implying from Jason.

She looked at me as if to say, "Now who's the phony bastard?"

She knew that even if you were an Eskimo you'd heard a lot about her. Clearly *I* was the phony bastard because we both were keenly aware Jason NEVER spoke her name the whole time I knew him, the phony bastard.

I mumbled something unintelligible to even me and made a much overdue exit.

It was a heady time being around such talent, but I recall being jealous of someone's performance in that class only once and that was while watching Sandler do a dramatic scene, of all things. I had no idea he was a standup comic at the time. It was obvious even then he had "it" in spades.

CHAPTER TEN

I'd been studying in Lynette's class for a couple of years when a guy I'd met once before at Miguel's showed up. We started hanging out incessantly and became best friends almost overnight. His name was Brandon Lee.

Yup, *that* Brandon Lee, son of Bruce Lee, who died just a few short years later on the set of *The Crow*.

The first time we'd met, I'd stopped by Miguel's Studio City pad and he was headed to a boxing match with Brandon. I knew Miggy was working with Brandon on a *Kung Fu* spinoff and I was pleasantly surprised to meet him.

Brandon greeted me with unusual enthusiasm, especially from someone who I considered kind of a star. I later found out he was so happy to meet me because he mistook me for Matthew Broderick whom I somewhat resembled at the time.

Once we went to see the film *Biloxi Blues* starring Matthew Broderick and as we exited, Brandon pretended I was Matthew and badgered me aggressively for an autograph until another patron broke it up, making Brandon ecstatic.

Those of us lucky enough to be close to him remember him as funny, generous, open minded, loyal, and very deep at times. He is one of those people (along with Mike Vendrell, his sensei) who made me feel I must've done something right to be in his presence and call him a friend.

I'm not sure why he picked me to be his running buddy, it seems he could have chosen to hang out with anyone. But we got on like a house on fire, and there was never a dull moment if you were up for what I called, "The Brandon Show." His energy was intense, and inexhaustible.

He matched wits with me with an insanely irreverent sense of humor but seemed far smarter. His place in Lynette's class was tenuous from the beginning as he was a natural iconoclast with authority issues, having once been thrown out of a private Catholic school for spitting out a communion wafer during services.

Maybe he didn't want to eat Jesus's flesh. So why did he want me to eat his? He voiced on more than one occasion that he wanted to be cooked up in a stew and eaten by his friends upon his demise. Thanks, Brandon.

His sexual tension and mistrust of authority came to a head, so to speak, when he decided to masturbate in front of the class as part of a "private moment" exercise onstage. It wasn't a private moment for long when he started pulling on "Little Elvis" like it was taffy. A flustered Lynette stopped the shenanigans and Brandon did a good job of trying to convince her that he was actually doing something artistic and worthy of exploration. Lynette was not amused.

Amazingly, she let him stay after that. Weeks later we did actually get thrown out of class after we cut out early one night. We thought we'd slip out unnoticed, but then Brandon had the bright idea of calling the theater pay phone to invite a cute girl in class, Holly Jones (who would later become John Lee Hancock's wife), to join us. Again, Lynette was not amused...

In the summer of 1988 I was going home to be with my high school running buddies, mostly drunk hippies, known as "the cousins" for our annual gathering called "The Wang Dang Doodle." It was being held at my friend David's house in Ennis, Texas, nearly an hour outside of Dallas. This was an excuse to drink and stay drunk for a whole weekend. Illicit substances were used in large quantities, but booze was our rocket fuel.

When I told Brandon that I was going to "the Doodle," he found it irresistible. His idea was to ride his Harley across the desert, *in July*. He, of course, wanted me to go with him, but I declined and took the wimp's way out on a jet. This did not slow down Brandon a bit. After getting directions to my house in Richardson, Texas from my brother Sherman, he promised to meet me there in a couple of days.

I was sitting in my childhood home around the kitchen table with my dad, Norvin, when I got a phone call that went exactly like this:

"Hello?"

"I'm going to cut your brother's head off and hold it up to a mirror so he can see the surprised look on his face."

"I take it you're lost."

Thankfully, it only took us a minute to figure out where he was. My dad suggested Brandon stay put and we'd go get him and have him follow us home. He was clearly in no mental condition to be driving around lost.

We jumped into my dad's canary yellow 1959 Thunderbird and took off for a Denny's in Garland, a short drive away. When we got there Brandon was smiling and happy, dressed in a dirty wife beater and even dirtier jeans with reverse raccoon eyes where his goggles had covered his face. I was pretty damn happy and amazed to see him. He got on his hog and followed us home. Dad was no fan of motorcycles and had Brandon park it in our backyard. Of course, we ended up driving around on it anyway. Once we came in from a ride and dad had come home in our absence and was sitting in the living room. I literally used Brandon as a human shield as we walked past my father and his disapproving gaze.

The weekend came and we made the drive to Ennis. Brandon was giddy at the prospect of unbridled mayhem in the ungodly Texas heat and he made sure everyone was going to have a memorable time by bringing out industrial size quantities of magic mushrooms.

Oh boy, here we go.

We got out to Davy's farm, and before you knew it my friends took to Brandon like he was one of ours and Brandon fit right in. These guys knew how to throw a party and Brandon knew how to end one.

Sherman had foolishly told Brandon that he'd gotten full insurance coverage on his rental car. Brandon took this as a challenge, and the next thing Sherman saw was someone driving through a field with Brandon "surfing" on the hood of the car leaving huge boot-shaped dents in it and cracking the windshield. The rental place must've been overjoyed. (This was twenty years before *Jackass*.)

There was a fishpond that in retrospect was probably chock full of cottonmouth snakes, but no one seemed to mind or got bitten. Not that anyone would've noticed a deadly snake bite. We had bigger fish to fry. Drunk "goat ropers" as we came to be, were lolling around in the pond and unintentionally swallowing the water in a vain effort to stave off the unholy heat. It didn't work.

Once everyone was dealing with alcohol poisoning *and* dehydration, it was a perfect time for Brandon to pull out the 'shrooms. BAD IDEA!

Brandon was always searching for a way make palatable something that quite literally tastes like SHIT. His preferred method at this time was making it into a tea. While it eventually had the desired effect, shit tea is still shitty. No one seemed to mind, however, and it seems most everyone partook of the potent brew.

The day slowly, *very slowly*, turned to night and that's when things got really weird. My friends started acting strangely (or normal for people *blazing on 'shrooms)*. There weren't a lot of responsible adults there at this time, so the creepiness factor was off the charts. Your mind starts making huge leaps of reasoning and judgement. The fact that Ennis, Texas, for example, is home to an enormous particle accelerator just miles from where we were *tripping balls* (as the kids say), seemed to be in the back of my mind and I gave it some significance. What about, I have no idea. Like I said, no one was thinking correctly.

My now-deceased friend Drew was making some God-awful references to the movie *The Shining* by repeating, "RED RUM, RED RUM," over and over. This did not have a calming effect. More on *The Shining* later.

Next thing you knew, our buddy Tony was so out of it he couldn't talk anymore, but at least he was conscious and semi-responsive. People started to get upset but I wasn't alarmed and knew he'd eventually come out of it, which he did.

A much bigger concern for me was Brandon had taken me aside after seeing what happened to Tony and claimed that he overheard my friends plotting to kill him for what he did to Tony, all of which was bullshit and I knew it at the time. But the fact that Brandon was suffering from paranoid delusions did not help matters.

Now came the coup de grace (defined as a death blow to a severely wounded animal or person). Brandon said that he and his dad were *Werewolves*. This was bad. Now, I can't say that I believed him but in my state I couldn't really know. Look who we are talking about, after all.

This was my signal to get Brandon the fuck out of there. Then Brandon announced that he was a time traveler, and he gave me a twig to hang onto while I went and got the car and a driver, as I was in no condition to take the wheel. The twig had zero significance but was just another way for Brandon to mess with my head, I was sure. However, I considered it a bad omen when I dropped the twig by accident and couldn't find it. And I hate bad omens.

It wasn't too long before I wrangled the only sober person I could find, the noble Paul Hoyt, a close cousin and the only sane person in sight.

We got into the car and took off for where I last saw Brandon. Of course he was gone, and we spent the next few minutes driving up and down dirt roads in search of this maniac.

The visual of him half lurching, half running out of the bushes and in front of our car was truly frightening. Torn shirt, bleeding from scratches, looking wild-eyed and Manson-like, we got him into the car. We should have locked him in the trunk and ran. Instead, we decided to drive the hour to Richardson and drop him at my parents' house. I knew he wouldn't mess with Norvin if he had one functioning brain cell left. In retrospect, I was right but I was taking a huge risk.

So we started down the two-lane road to get to the 75 freeway and it was bad. Brandon had seemingly lost the ability to speak. We stupidly put him in the front passenger seat, and he started grabbing the wheel from Paul and steering us into oncoming traffic. We should've pulled over then and there, but we trudged on. Things calmed down some until we hit Saturday night Dallas traffic and I had to take a leak. Although I correctly sensed disaster, I decided to not piss my pants. Wish I'd had my Depends on that night.

We pulled over at the worst place possible, Greenville Avenue on a Saturday night. Anyone familiar with Greenville Avenue in Dallas knows that it's been famous for its bars and nightlife since the 1920s. This night it was hopping. We pulled over to some yuppie bar so I could use the bathroom. The sidewalks were crowded and I plowed through the throng to go inside. I returned to witness my worst fears fully realized. Brandon was on the hood of the car and Paul was talking to him like Jane Goodall speaking to an unruly chimp. Brandon was having none of it. He'd grabbed the windshield wipers and was trying to pull one off. A crowd was gathering to watch and it was becoming a spectacle. God only knows how we managed to get him back in the car and on the road to Dad's house. We dropped him off in my old bedroom and headed back to the party.

Somehow the evening turned to day and with not one serious casualty, save for my feelings. I was pretty distraught at the thought of Brandon being so reckless. I felt he should've realized more than anyone what a vulnerable state I was in to be messing with me on such a deep level. And I did believe he was in control of his actions, evidenced by the fact that he was no more trouble once back at my parents' house, as I'd hoped.

Brandon was an avid reader and at the time the two books he was delving into were *The Holy Bible* and Stephen King's *The Shining*. There was no correlation, or so I thought at the time, but clearly Brandon was interested in the supernatural.

I had a come to Jesus meeting with him that Monday morning. "How could you do this?"

"Do what, Slim"?

So I let him have it over being so irresponsible and putting me in such a horrible position. I hadn't known him for long at this point and I was questioning the wisdom of continuing our friendship. And then I said something that seems ridiculous in retrospect, because it was.

"If you keep reading *The Bible* and *The Shining* at the same time, you'll get what you're asking for."

Brandon had never heard anything this ridiculous and let me know it. Anyway I expressed myself, he apologized and we moved on. That Christmas he ended up giving me the Bible he was reading as a gift with this inscription on the title page:

Bill Allen

"WARNING: Do not read in conjunction with *The Shining* or you'll get what you're asking for, MISTER!"

Brandon soon became a part of my gang, a ready-made posse. He met George Davis, who was impressed not only with Brandon but also his pedigree and they became good drinking buddies. John liked Brandon enough to make him a part of our theatre company and got down to writing what would become the play, *Fulfed Beast,* a four-person prison drama for George, Brandon, Tom Kurlander, and me.

John did a brilliant job tailoring the roles to the actors. We were all already in the company except for Tom, who I knew from acting class and who joined the cast after the script was completed. I had to push John to give him the role after George Davis intentionally intimidated the crap out of Tom during the audition, just because he could.

It was a one-act play that took place in a Hollywood jail cell. I played a belligerent soap opera actor, Brandon and Tom portrayed small time thugs, while George Davis played a bonafide murderer. He played the crap out of that role, and the air was electrified when he took the stage. I was able to witness greatness up close. Thanks, George.

Brandon was very good, too, but he required a lot of special care, analyzing everything to death, picking the script apart in the quest of "great art," and grating on everyone's nerves. John had made the mistake of telling Brandon the play was about his character when really it was an ensemble piece, so Brandon took liberties because of that. He had a way of pulling focus anyway. Brandon seemed to revel in tweaking everyone's nerves, and getting everyone's attention, even if it was negative.

Since he was playing a street thug, he decided to panhandle and make enough money to stay in a fleabag motel at Hollywood Blvd. and Bronson Ave. (a not-so-great part of town), all in the name of research. Pretty brave stuff, in retrospect.

As he told us later, there was no bathroom in the rooms so when he got up in the middle of the night to take a leak, he walked out into the hall naked and the door closed behind him, locking him out. He decided to simply kick the door down, and promptly grabbed his clothes and ran. That was a typical day for him in many ways in that he seemed to take things to the extreme in everything he did.

The run of *Fulfed* was short as planned, with only a handful of performances. But it was obvious we had a hit on our hands and we hoped to move it to a larger theater. John crafted a movie script based on the play, and while it had the smell of success, John and the cast (myself included) were irritated beyond measure by Brandon's offstage antics. He was so morbidly self-absorbed during rehearsals that it became about placating Brandon instead of working on the show. So John told Brandon that if the play were restaged, his part would be recast.

This was devastating to young Brandon. He announced to me one night after a few too many, that if it ever was staged again he would, "burn the theater to the ground." I took this declaration as a good sign that he wasn't actually *already* setting things on fire.

Fortunately, he never got the chance to fulfill that promise as we never did put it up again.

Much to his credit, when Brandon started to take big industry meetings looking for vehicles for him to star in he took John Lee along with him to pitch scripts and acted as if nothing had happened, a generous gesture John appreciated a lot.

CHAPTER ELEVEN

Another show we staged around the same time was a quasi-musical John Lee wrote called *A Riff for Emily*. My brother, Sherman, both an actor and musician, took the lead role. He played a struggling blues guitarist and I was cast as his heavy-metal loving harmonica player. (No, they don't actually exist!)

For the show we put together a ragtag blues band called The Pipefitters. After our first preview, John thought the show was not up to snuff, and he pulled the plug after one performance. But that show had a long-lasting effect on my life anyway.

Though the play folded before it began, The Pipefitters stayed together and we started playing many of the coolest clubs around the Sunset Strip, including The Rainbow Room, The Troubadour, Club Lingerie, Black and Blue, and The China Club, to name a few. Lou Diamond Phillips graciously let us set up our band equipment in his sprawling Hollywood Hills home and would often find himself grabbing the mic after he downed a few, so soon became an official member.

This was around the time that he split with his first wife, Julie Cypher, when she left him for

Grammy-winning singer/songwriter, Melissa Etheridge. Melissa lived right up the block from Lou, and they all remained friends for some time, so Melissa became a fixture at the house and sat in on many of our gigs.

I recall Jon Bon Jovi hanging out with the band and jamming and doing a nationally syndicated radio show with Lou. Before Lou left for the studio to do the interview, I gave him a cassette demo tape of the band, just in case. Well, Jon went on the air and gave the host a talk up about the band, going on and on about how good we sounded. I seem to recall a comparison to THE BEATLES. The interviewer then put in the tape only on the opposite side of the demo track, and a dry drum and vocal track came on that was NOT meant for public consumption. It sounded not good at all, in fact. I thought it was hysterical. Sherman, our lead guitarist, not so much.

Our good friend, rock guitar god, Steve Lukather (of Toto fame, who also played the guitar riff on *Beat it* by Michael Jackson) would come to our gigs and sat in dozens of times, once even on drums. He provided constant entertainment as the funniest guy in the room, and a true master of his instrument. We remain friends today and he has to be the coolest guy in the music business, if not the most prolific. Look up his discography and set your face to shock.

My RAD Career

I didn't have a bike as a kid, but I did a lot of this in the early '80s

1982 - Clowning Around with George Clooney and Miguel Ferrer on the set of "And They're Off"

My RAD Career

Jose Ferrer and me - this moment captures the most and the least experienced actors on the planet.

Bill Allen

1982 – With Danger Boy, George Clooney

My RAD Career

1983 – Robert Altman and me on the set of Streamers

Bill Allen

My acting coach, Bryan, and me

My RAD Career

Jose catching air

Bill Allen

Hell Track in action

My RAD Career

Eddie, Jose, and me

Bill Allen

Bart and Me

My RAD Career

Lori and Me

Bill Allen

Lori and Me

My RAD Career

Jack Weston, Alfie Wise and Me

Jamie, Marta, and one of the twins

My RAD Career

Goofing off in cast van

Bill Allen

1985- With Keenan Wynn on the set of "Hyper Sapien"

My RAD Career

Rich doing his thing

Bill Allen

Touring for RAD

My RAD Career

Touring for RAD

Bill Allen

Miguel, Bill Mumy and me

My RAD Career

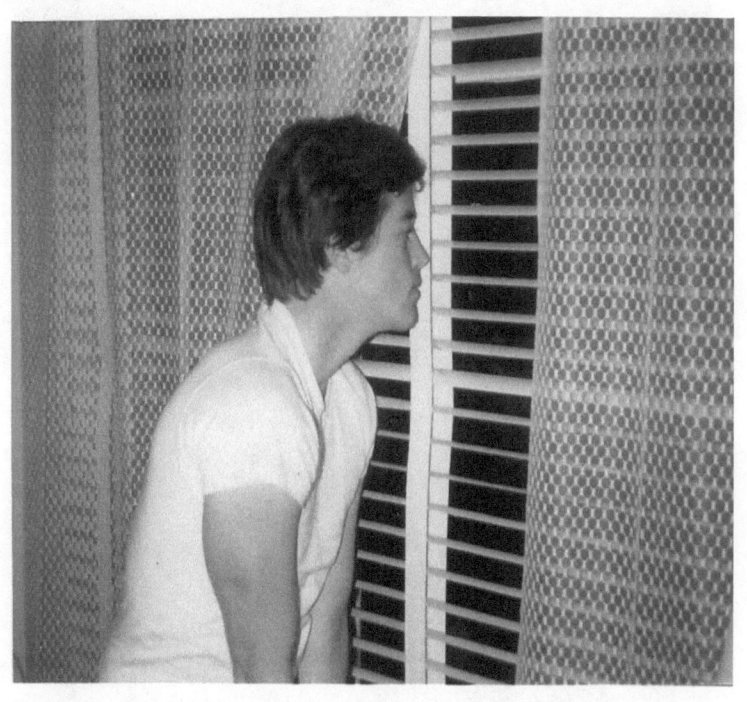

Watching the parade go by without me

1987 – Big Lou and me at the La Bamba premiere

Willie Dixon and me at the La Bamba premiere

Bill Allen

*Roy Orbison and me at the
La Bamba premiere*

1988ish – With Michael J. Fox on the set of Family Ties

Bill Allen

With Marc Price on the set of Family Ties
(check out Michael J. Fox smoking and photo bombing us)

My RAD Career

*1989 – Jungle Training for
Born On The Fourth of July*

1988 – with my buddy, guitar god Bugs Henderson

1989 - Sherman and George Davis

Bill Allen

1993 - The Crow Car

My RAD Career

1992 - A Pipefitters publicity shot

Bill Allen

1993 – Livin' large at Farm Aid

Carol and me, our American Indian wedding
Photo by Joseph Kaiser

2012 – Daniel Tosh and me

My RAD Career

2012 - Lou, Sherman, and Steve Lukather and me

Bill Allen

Hal and me at the RAD 25th reunion

My RAD Career

Jose Yanez, Eddie Fiola, and me almost thirty years later...
photo by Tony Donaldson

Bill Allen

Eddie Fiola, Martin Aparijo, and me holding this very book

My RAD Career

I do a lot of this...

2014 – Carol and Me

CHAPTER TWELVE

The first person to actually push me in front of a mic to play harmonica was Bill Mumy of *Lost in Space* fame. Miguel and Bill had been friends for decades, and I was especially happy to meet Bill, as I was a big fan of his growing up. It was a bit strange for me, too, because as children we were both red-headed boys named Billy, so I'd always felt strangely connected to him.

He starred in a *Twilight Zone* episode, his character's name was Billy, and he was told by his dead grandmother to commit suicide. It was beyond creepy and had a hold on my young psyche. Because of this, he was someone I'd thought about more than the average TV viewer in the '60s, so it was surreal to finally meet him.

He lived in idyllic Laurel Canyon and had the first real home studio I ever saw. He's had a prolific musical career which included touring with the rock band America and teen idol Shaun Cassidy, and being half of the infamous Barnes and Barnes that made novelty records in the '70s including "Fish Heads," a song heavily featured on a favorite radio program of mine when I was growing up, *The Dr. Demento Show*.

So for *the* Bill Mumy to welcome me to play a few cuts on his CD, *Golden Days*, was something I treasured. I got to play with Weird Al Yankovic on the accordion, trading licks, which was downright surreal. The CD is *Golden Age* and is still available on Mumy's website, www.billmumy.com. It's pretty good, too.

Bill had a band made up of comic book artists, and they called themselves *Seduction of the Innocent* (a reference to early comic book warnings), which included Miguel on drums. We actually played some gigs, the most memorable being at San Diego Comic Con. I have not been back since, but it stands out in my mind due to the fact that hanging with Bill and Miguel at a sci-fi convention (Miguel had been in *Robocop* by this time) was like going to a rock show with Elvis.

I asked Miguel how people treated him in the comic book world and he replied, "Slim, I'm a God" and he wasn't exaggerating.

One of the first things I saw at Comic Con was Mumy's friend, Mark Hamill (aka Luke Skywalker) in sunglasses, trying to avoid being recognized, while he sold comic books out of cardboard boxes to accommodate his appetite for better comics. I was truly in the land of the weird. We also played the Oakland Comic Con, and somehow I convinced Miguel to let me drive him there from L.A. in the middle of the night before the gig in his Porsche 911. He passed out in the passenger seat while I drove at light speed. He came so close to death that night and never realized it.

Miguel, being a drummer, forgot his cymbals, the only thing he was supposed to bring. So well after midnight, we put in a call to Brandon from the Porsche's prehistoric car phone. Brandon, we found out later, was in the middle of someone at the time, foolishly picked up the phone. Miguel demanded he fly up and meet us, but first he must go to his house and "look for the cymbals." Brandon mistook "cymbals" for "symbols" and went over to Miggy's to look for hieroglyphs on the walls. He did make it up to Oakland the next day with said cymbals in hand, and the weekend stands out for this cute story...

At the gig we enjoyed a reception akin to the treatment the Beatles received at Shea Stadium, however I was humbled when a legendary writer for comic books, Peter David, was invited up to play with us. Despite weighing in at about 450 lbs., wearing sweatpants and a stuffed animal on his head, and being a worse singer than he was a dresser, the audience of hundreds of sweaty and uncomfortable social outcasts went crazy for him. And I mean NUTS!! So much for wowing 'em with my stupid kazoo.

The after party proved to be even stranger than the gig. I walked in with Miguel, Brandon, and the rest of the band, sans Mumy. The room was crowded and music was playing, but there was zero interaction going on between the people in the room. For many, some in comic book character costumes – Superman, Aquaman, Wonder Woman, etc., this was obviously the only time they ventured out of the house all year long and they seemed extremely uncomfortable.

I remember at least one guy in the corner engrossed in his *Wall Street Journal*, as though alone in his living room, while the rest were about as charming. We started talking to one heavy-set gal who was wearing an unfortunate dress covered by an even more unfortunate satin jacket that was popular at the time, with Spiderman embroidered on the back. We soon started referring to her as "Spider Woman."

Brandon seemed to be having a private moment with Spidey, and she got very quiet and uncomfortable as Mumy walked in. Mumy, sensing that something significant had just transpired, asked Miguel what was going on. Miggy, in an oh-so-subtle foghorn-like voice (the equivalent of any normal person screaming at the top of his lungs) announced, "BRANDON ASKED SPIDER WOMAN IF SHE'D GO IN THE BATHROOM AND BLOW HIM!"

Now, this got all the nerds' attention, and not in a good way.

They were clearly not used to this kind of outburst. Frankly neither was I, however my reaction was to laugh like a hyena with rabies. The nerds' response was mostly to flee and hide. Spidey burst into tears and ran out of the room, clearly not wanting to "blow" anyone.

Hey, I told you it was a cute story.

My RAD Career

This was about the time that The Pipefitters were getting some traction, and we started touring extensively all over the U.S. and Canada, and even made an appearance on MTV. Because of Lou's stardom, we were able to get gigs that many signed artists would've died for.

We were on the constant hunt for a record deal and spent quite a bit of Lou's money cutting demos. Melissa even came and played guitar on a track, and I was awestruck at her rock-solid rhythm playing.

Because of the ever-elusive record deal, we never put a CD out, although we did play on the soundtrack of a film Lou directed, *Sioux City*. Now I find it humorous that we played hundreds of gigs, and never sold one CD or even played "La Bamba." We were yearning for some street cred and wanted to portray ourselves as a band that didn't need to ride on the success of one song, while most bands would've killed to be associated with a recognizable hit in their set list.

Not us. Heck, Lou didn't do any actual singing on the *La Bamba* soundtrack anyway. That was David Hidalgo of Los Lobos. Well, the schoolteacher in Lake Charles, Louisiana, couldn't give two craps Lou had lip-synced. She and her drunken friends wanted Chaves to sing the only song they've ever heard him sing, an international hit on par with *Gangnam Style*. But, no, despite the audience demanding it at every gig, The Pipefitters were too precious to do that. But we *would* sing some love song we'd penned about some chick none of us gave a crap about anymore, or who Lou happened to be banging.

It didn't seem to matter. Lou was such a big deal at the time, no one cared that we didn't have a record deal or even a song the local radio stations could play to promote our gigs.

We got some national exposure by playing about a dozen times on a TNN show, *Nashville Now*, a very popular variety show for the *Hee Haw* crowd, hosted by a guy named Ralph Emery. He was used to talking to Kitty Wells and Minnie Pearl and was old enough to be around at the invention of not only country music, but our country, period.

He didn't really get our humor. Lou even guest hosted one time, and we concocted a bit we didn't much plan out beforehand, and I had forgotten about it until Lou said we'd do it on live TV, minutes before airtime, and we'd "wing it." This should've set off some warning bells in my head. It didn't.

The bit involved me dressing up like Ralph's sidekick on the show, a redneck puppet named Shotgun Red. At some point in the middle of the show, I popped out from under the desk with a straw hat and stupid bandana and red ball nose, and Lou introduced me to the crowd as "Shotgun Slim."

I thought it would be funny if Shotgun Slim mistakes Lou for the real Richie Valens, the character he portrayed in *La Bamba*. I told him he looked great and commented that plane wrecks must be a good weight loss program. Crickets. (In case you didn't know, Richie Valens died in a plane crash with Buddy Holly, making this joke extremely thoughtful and classy of me.)

It got even worse when I decided to recreate the scene in *Young Guns II* where Christian Slater puts a knife through Lou's arm. So I pulled out a real knife and began to approach Lou ominously. This lent a Kafkaesque quality to the show, in front of an audience that had no idea who Kafka was. (It's likely you don't either, because really—who does?)

Thankfully, we cut to a commercial before I had to stab him to end the bit. A friend of mine was there that night, playing on the same episode with his band, The Wagoneers. They had a real Buddy Holly quality to their music. Monty, the lead singer, was actually friends with Buddy's widow and told me she was planning to watch the show that night and would love the joke about the plane wreck that killed her husband. Nice.

Early on in my musical career, I met the love of my life at a Pipefitters gig, playing at a friend's backyard party. Carol made the first move (SWEAR TO GOD) I found out later, 'cause I was her type. (She was a big Michael J. Fox fan.) She was a professional dog walker (they have those out here) and because of that, had a kind disposition and a great BUTT!

It was only later that she became a Vedic astrologer and relationship coach (loveisinthestars.com), thereby turning me into a reluctant believer (and making me feel like a character in *Spinal Tap*).

In fact, in the beginning I was so horrified that she wanted to study astrology (it didn't help matters that her first "teacher" had other ideas beyond tutoring her), it contributed to a breakup we had for several years.

She eventually grew to tolerate me and is now convinced I'm a great guy. (Stockholm Syndrome perhaps?) I try as best I can to keep that charade going, and the reward is living with and loving the best person I've ever met.

The band continued to tour and make movies at the same time. I worked on all of Lou's early efforts as a writer/director, among them a film called *Dangerous Touch* about a mobster who tells his troubles to a shrink. This was a decade before *The Sopranos* or *Analyze This*. I was also fortunate to have a nice role in *Sioux City*, a good film about an Indian (Lou) who gets into trouble by finding out about his past. I play a bad cop. Those are the most fun roles to play. I even get thrown off a cliff by Gary Farmer, a fine performer.

Some of the highlights I enjoyed as a touring musician included playing Farm Aid with The Pipefitters. Little did I know that Carol, who I'd already temporarily split with, was picking up a dog at someone's house who happened to be watching the telecast when we were announced, so she saw us on TV in front of tens of thousands of people, and I had the best FU moment of my life but wasn't even aware of it until she told me years later.

Another highlight was playing in the glorious Gorge amphitheater in George, Washington, and touring stadiums with Billy Ray Cyrus for a few dates. This was decades before anyone heard of Miley Cyrus. Billy Ray was still touring on the strength of "Achy Breaky Heart," widely regarded as one of the worst songs of all time.

The actual worst song of all time is "Afternoon Delight" by Starland Vocal Band.
(www.youtube.com/watch?v= Fz1ex78QeQI.)

While "Achy Breaky" is bad, it's not close to the worst song of all time. I say that because while The Pipefitters toured with Billy Ray, he would invite us onstage to sing backup on the song for the finale of his show that was, of course, "Achy Breaky" and I came to realize when singing it and shaking what my mama gave me, I LOVE THIS SONG. It helps when you have 15,000 screaming fans at your feet. I advise only singing that song under those conditions.

CHAPTER THIRTEEN

It was around 1990 that we received the horrible news that our dear friend, George Davis, had contracted ALS, Lou Gehrig's disease. ALS is a quick spreading disease that eats away muscle tissue, soon rendering the victim wheelchair bound, with death coming not long after from slow suffocation.

This news put a damper on me and my friends' belief that we were invincible. We clearly weren't if the strongest and most talented among us was being taken away so horribly. George's illness affected Brandon greatly. He didn't speak of it much, but the blow was devastating to him and I'm sure it brought up the feelings of losing his father again. He even started a college fund for George's infant son, Tucker.

This was about the time that John Lee was coming into his own as a writer, and we all felt he was on his way. He'd gotten a small company to bankroll a movie that he'd originally written for George to star in, but he was just too ill to make but a cameo appearance.

Vaya con Dios was shot in New Mexico, my first introduction to a place that would become significant in my life. It was a good effort for a tiny-budgeted movie, and a good time was had by all.

It was John Lee's next script that kicked open the door to Hollywood for him, where he's remained (having written and/or directed and produced a bunch of films, including *The Rookie, The Alamo, The Blind Side, Saving Mr. Banks,* and more). *A Perfect World* was written and John was able to get it to a fine producer I've since had the privilege to work for, Polly Platt, and before you knew it folks like Spielberg, Barry Levinson and Eastwood wanted to direct. Kevin Costner was red hot at the time, and he signed on in the lead role with Eastwood directing.

So much for our little film production adventures—John Lee was onto the big time and hasn't looked back.

In 1988 I had a job in North Carolina in a TV movie playing a troubled kid who, on an outing with his buddies, throws some rocks at an Amish family that kill their infant son. It was clumsily titled, *A Stoning in Fulham County*.

I was happy to get the gig and it had some really good cast members including Ken Olin, Ron Perlman, and Noble Willingham. I was playing one of a small gang of young thugs, and they brought in one other actor from L.A. for our gang, while the other two kids were hired locally. I was in my room looking at the call sheet and decided to call the other L.A. guy, an actor I'd heard of - some kid named Brad Pitt.

I called him on the hotel line and said we should hang out. I went to his room to meet him. This was only a couple of weeks after I'd crashed an audition for a biopic about James Dean, an opportunity coveted by any young actor. I'd bleached my hair, worked up a pretty awful imitation, I'm sure, and never got a second look much less a call back. When I went to Brad's room and he opened the door, standing before me was a modern incarnation of Dean.

So I walked in and the first thing out of my mouth was, "So, how did the James Dean audition go?"

He lit up like a bulb. Very excited, he told me how the producers flipped for him and it looked pretty good. He never asked how I knew he'd auditioned for the role. As it turned out, he later got the gig (no surprise) but the production never happened.

In spite of this, he was hard not to like, being from the Midwest and all. We got along great and formed a clique with the two other guys in our movie "gang."

We were again given the nickname the Bad Boys (I couldn't seem to get away from that persona for some reason) and had a lot of time to hang out and tour around North Carolina. We became good friends with the local casting lady, Pam Plumber, who became somewhat of a den mother to us.

I can tell you after going to Bummer's restaurant for livermush and eggs with Brad a bunch of times, the livermush made more of a stir than he did. I don't recall our waitress, Madge, throwing her granny panties on his plate of grits as she served 'em. He was a twenty-five-year old pre-fame Brad Pitt, yet I never once saw anyone faint in his presence. Showbiz is a profession akin to the fairytale, *The Emperor's New Clothes*. Now people will bid thousands of dollars on a jar of air bottled near his presence.

We went to some movies while on location including one of the worst films of the eighties, *Cocktail*. It's a howlingly atrocious movie starring Tom Cruise. We were goofing on Tom's last name and decided that Brad would never make it with a ridiculous name like Pitt, so we dubbed him "Brad Turbo" or "Turbo" for short, and that was his nickname for the remainder of our friendship.

After going to see several films while we were on location, Brad would comment that his actress girlfriend at the time had "dated" about every other actor that came on screen to the point that I figured she must've been behind the desk at the SAG credit union handing out blumpkins with every transaction.

I still remember him telling me right at the time it happened the now famous story of when he dated Robin Givens who he'd met while filming the sitcom, *Head of the Class*. He and Robin came home to her condo one night and when she looked out the window she saw her ex, Mike Tyson, in a Mercedes limo outside at the curb.

She hysterically told Brad who fled upstairs (never go up in a chase!) and he watched his life flash before his eyes for hours while "Iron Mike" waited outside all night long before leaving. It seemed to me that Brad liked drama in his relationships. I can't say what he likes now.

The writers of the TV movie wrote in a scene for Brad at the end of the script where he had to come clean with his mother. He was the only one in the gang who got an extra scene, and after seeing it when it aired I knew he deserved it. I was shocked at the depth he had in that one stupid scene, never expecting this pretty boy/business school (almost) graduate from Springfield to have the real "goods."

We remained friends after the shoot for some time, a rarity in Hollywood. I invited him up to Lou's house for our weekly Monday night poker game where he became a regular and he came out to several Pipefitters gigs.

Of course, Brandon was also a part of the regular crowd but Lou was the big dog back then, and Brad was pretty star-struck, as I recall. He was also enamored of one of Lou's costars in *Young Guns*, Dermot Mulroney, a regular at Lou's house with his girlfriend and now ex-wife, Catherine Keener, whom I'd worked with on the TV show, *O'HARA*. Brad had even talked about being a fan of Dermot's while we were in North Carolina. So meeting him was a big thrill and I believe they became good friends after that.

I've only seen Brad once since his career blew up...

My RAD Career

He was to appear at a screening of *The Curious Story of Benjamin Button* in Westwood and I decided I'd try and get his attention. I'm usually pretty fearless in situations like that. So about halfway through the movie I heard an uproar in the lobby so I figured our boy must've arrived. I found out the next day in the press that Brad showed up in a goofy mustache and pork pie hat, not looking like a *People* magazine cover shoot. Security at the theater didn't recognize him and got into a scrape with his handlers. A melee ensued. I'm sure this had something to do with his state of mind by the time I saw him.

So I marched out of the screening and everything seemed normal, except for the security guarding the bathroom staircase. Bingo. I walked past and up the stairs, and there was Brad talking to a couple of people in line, waiting to kiss his ring.

God, they were laying it on thick, as if his urine could cure polio. Now, I knew he was gonna recognize me. Lou said he'd asked about me not too long before that when he'd bumped into him somewhere. When I got to the head of the line, he was drinking a beer with his right hand (in a movie theater?) and shook my hand with his left. Okay, I got it. He shakes a thousand hands a night and keeps his right hand germ free. But it was still a little creepy. I bet he lets Bono germ up his mitt any time he wants. He seemed hardly excited to see me after nearly twenty years.

I steered the conversation toward Brandon as I was writing about him at the time, and Brad told me a story about Brandon telling him he didn't expect to live long, not unusual for Brandon. Brad introduced me to David Fincher and we took a two-minute ride down memory lane before I high-tailed it outta there.

Elia Kazan said that the more rich and famous people become, the more they take on the appearance of wax fruit. And although I'm a huge fan of his talent, Brad's no different, at least from what I saw that night. Is he too fabulous, or am I jealous? You be the judge. Seriously, he was probably worn out from too much living. Hard to blame him.

I only saw Clooney once after he got huge. It was at a screening of *Michael Clayton* at the TV academy. Carol was with me and came back from the restroom and said George was in the lobby. When she'd introduced herself as "Slim's wife" he told her I was the reason he'd moved to L.A. (Where's my Thank You yacht?)

So I went out to say hi and he was as cool as ever. He didn't seem to feel the need to be above it all. He was happy to see me and sealed my man crush on him forever.

CHAPTER FOURTEEN

I could've been Charlie Sheen. No, really. Martin was never my dad or anything, but I almost got the role that made Charlie famous. It was the eighties and I was auditioning a lot in those days. I got a call about a Vietnam movie called *The Platoon*. It was being directed by a then little-known writer named Oliver Stone. Somehow my manager had gotten the script and I got to read it before I met with Oliver. I was under strict orders to not say that I had - no one on my team was supposed to have at that time.

Oliver's only claim to fame was as a writer on a little-known horror film called *The Hand*, starring Michael Caine. (Did you ever notice if you say Michael Caine it sounds like Michael Caine saying, "My cocaine"? Try it.)

This movie was spoofed on SCTV as *My Bloody Hand*. So needless to say, he didn't have the clout he does now, so I wasn't intimidated at all. However, it was an amazing script and a leading part I could sink my teeth into and I'd always been obsessed with military roles, so I wanted in on this one.

Excited, I showed up at Oliver's suite at the Westwood Marquis. After a quick chat, he asked if I wanted to read. So without even handing me a script, he started reading a scene with me. I replied as best I could, remembering lines that I'd read the night before. A page or two in, he looked at me to say my next line that I didn't have memorized. I told him he never gave me pages to read from. He looked surprised. "How did you follow along?" I said I just followed what he was doing. The dude nearly shit his pants. He was astounded I could come up with his dialogue BEFORE reading it, which of course I hadn't.

Next thing I knew, he excused himself to go into his bedroom and call my manager. I basically had the job, right then and there. I was thrilled. This was my big break at last!

Then I starred in the movie that won the Oscar for best picture. Wait a second. I guess that wasn't me. What happened, you ask?

The original producer was a character named Dino De Laurentis (otherwise known as Dino De HORRENDOUS). He pulled out of the deal (smart move on his part. Yes, that was sarcasm) and Oliver went and shot *El Salvador* with James Woods.

When he came back to shoot the now simply titled *Platoon* a couple of years later, Charlie Sheen was cast as the lead and I was chopped liver. At the time Charlie had one credit in a starring role in a movie no one saw. His main claim to war movie fame was his dad starred in *Apocalypse Now*. *Platoon* was Charlie's launching pad and for so many others, too. It's a veritable who's who of stars before they became stars. Watch *Platoon* today and you'll be shocked by the line-up: Johnny Depp, Willem Defoe, Forest Whitaker, Eric Stoltz, and the list goes on.

It was in about 1990 that I was cast in Oliver's film, *Born on the Fourth of July* with Tom Cruise. I was to play the soldier Tom's character accidentally shoots with "friendly fire" during combat, and whose memory haunts him for the rest of the film.

I went through weeks of Marine jungle warfare training by former Marine Captain Dale Dye, who trained all the actors for all of Oliver's Vietnam movies, not to mention *Saving Private Ryan*, among others. Dale did three tours in Nam, as did several of the former officers he had with him. Except for the Corpsman or medic as we know them, they were all killers of men. I came to gain immense respect for all of them. Most people would've considered their abilities to be superhuman and, in fact, they were.

There was a short rehearsal in NYC before the shoot began. To sit at a table read with Tom Cruise, Willem Defoe, and the amazing cast Oliver brought on board gave me goosebumps. It just so happened that Brandon was in town so I invited him to have dinner with the troops, Tom included.

By this time I was fairly comfortable around Tom, so I wasn't expecting Brandon to be so dour when he showed up at the restaurant. I had not seen the side of Brandon that wasn't "Mr. Life of the Party." It took a minute to snap to the fact that

Brandon was clearly intimidated or jealous of Tom or both, while I wasn't at all.

We were eating dinner and at one point a sweet girl came up to Tom and asked for an autograph and he was totally cool and accommodating. A few minutes later, Brandon asked me under his breath, "Wouldn't it be funny if I put some girl up to coming over and asking for your autograph?" I told him no, because it wouldn't have been funny. It was then that somebody piped up and announced to Tom that Brandon was Bruce's Lee's son.

Tom was gobsmacked and practically launched over the table to shake Brandon's hand and tell him it was an honor to meet him. This made Brandon relax a little, and once the alcohol kicked in, the party was on. We ended up having cab races to a pool hall where I watched a hosed Brandon get his clock cleaned. Brandon was good, but I'd bragged to one of the actors that Brandon could take him. Turns out the other guy was a hustler and took Brandon for all he had that night. Funny.

The training for the movie began in some godforsaken forest outside of Houston, Texas. Due to a mix up by the production company, I landed at the wrong airport and had to take an expensive cab ride to the hotel that was conveniently located right by the airport where I *should have landed,* in the Houston area. By the time I got to the hotel, I was pissed and hours late. I could tell when I walked through the lobby in my Vietnam-era jungle boots that I was in the right place, thanks to the freshly shorn actors running around in fatigues.

My RAD Career

I was standing in line waiting to check in when a little Gunny Sargent walked up to me and asked if I was Bill Allen. When I answered in the affirmative, this guy went off in my face like a grenade. I saw myself as a professional actor filled with righteous indignation who needed to express my feelings, while too afraid to actually do so. He saw me as his new recruit he had to beat into shape. Turns out he was right.

He didn't care in the least that it was no fault of mine that I was late. He was not the type used to taking excuses, and he had no plans to start now with some "whiney, civilian puke actor." I got the distinct impression that if we were not in some swank hotel lobby, he'd have decked me like he clearly wanted to.

I came to actually like Gunny Thurman, but at that moment he had me fearing for what would happen when we broke camp the next day. The only thing he liked about me was the fact that I'd already gotten my own boots so I wouldn't have to waste his time picking out ones from the wardrobe department.

After I was sheared like a sheep, I remember going up to my room and freaking out that I was in over my head and calling my old man as though he could do something to help me. He couldn't. There was nothing I could do except show up and give it my best.

The next day was our first day out and we were ordered by Captain Dye to "Dig your home," that is, dig a shallow trench that you can sleep in, covered by your rain poncho in case of weather.

I was digging away when I heard Gunny Thurman calling for me, LOUD. The first thing any soldier will tell you is NEVER GO ANYWHERE WITHOUT YOUR RIFLE. I figured Gunny would kill me right then and there if I showed up without mine. Only problem was, I couldn't find it, and the more frantically I searched, the louder Gunny yelled. I was forced to give up and run over to Gunny empty-handed.

I knew this was gonna be bad. Remember, I was about to run up to a mass murderer who hated me and now had a reason to kill me. When I got there he happened to be standing right next to Tom, who was giving me the stink eye, too.

The first thing out of Gunny's mouth was, "Allen, WHERE'S YOUR RIFLE?"

He had me with that one.

"I don't know, Gunny."

"What the fuck do you mean, you don't know?"

He then produced my M1 carbine with a grenade launcher attached from behind his back. Someone had obviously turned it in, probably Tom, now that I think about it.

The screaming and humiliation seemed worse than if he'd killed me and "skull fucked me" like he threatened and clearly wanted to do. He somehow crowbarred in the fact that forty-eight thousand of his peers were killed in Nam, making me feel somehow responsible.

This guy was good.

Training included a couple of weeks in ungodly Texas heat, eighteen hours a day. We were being psychologically conditioned to hate and kill the enemy—the enemy being the Viet Cong for the movie's purposes, and we were training as if the Vietnam war was still raging.

Racism was part of the brain washing, and it works like you wouldn't believe. The Marine officers who trained us were used to turning farm boys into skilled killers in a few weeks, and let me tell you, they are the best in the world at this. They couldn't have cared less about a movie being shot, just that we got what they were teaching.

I decided that if I was going to be there, I was going to go all the way and see what was on the other side. That's how they got to me and most everyone they've ever trained.

There was a night where explosive charges were planted around our camp unbeknownst to us, right by our sleeping holes, while we were out training. About a half an hour after we laid down to get the two hours of sleep we were allowed per night, the charges started going off all around us, loud as cannon fire. Everyone was screaming to return fire, and even though we were firing blanks, it felt like we were fighting for our lives.

This little exercise made us feel as though we'd survived a truly traumatic experience, complete with mild PTSD symptoms.

I got to know Tom some during this time and he was a very good leader, able to let his guard down and just be one of the guys. He always picked up the check at dinner during the shoot and was very cool to work with. He invited the actors he trained with to his NYC apartment, which was not a dump.

He got in my face once during training, and it was right up there with any of the worst nights of my life.

It was our last exercise before leaving Texas, and we wanted it to go off without a hitch. It was a final exam of sorts. The war game involved doing reconnaissance during the day, to choose positions where we were told the "enemy" (actually the reserve Marines enlisted by Captain Dye) would most likely be walking through later, as well as choosing our positions for to execute a night ambush.

After lights out and eating our MREs (meals, ready to eat) we struck out to go to the positions we'd scouted earlier. Not far out of the tree line we were signaled to crouch down on our knees and watch out for "the enemy."

I knelt down on what happened to be a very soft pile of sand and took what comfort I could, as it was going to be a long night. I was already covered in painful chigger bite welts (microscopic insects had injected larvae into my skin the previous week and were now feeding off of me under my skin and were very painful and itchy). As it turns out, the sand pile I was sitting on happened to be a FIRE ANT HILL. By the time I realized my predicament, I was COVERED with stinging ants. This is fatal in some cases, and I was in danger of blood poisoning without speedy medical attention.

Right as I was going through my own personal ambush, we were given the sign to move out, and I did, all the while trying to get the ants off of me. I would've looked comical had anyone been able to see me, but it was a moonless night, so the only way to detect me frantically trying to get rid of the damn ants was the noise I was making. Before I knew it, Tom, who was the squad leader, got up in my grill, freaking out as to why I was making all the commotion.

I didn't even tell him, I just tried to keep it down until we reached our positions. Before long we were at the place where we were to wait for "the enemy." We were placed five or so feet apart in a row of bushes. I was left by myself to agonize over the red ant and chigger party that was going on all over my body. Even though there were guys on either side of me practically within arm's reach, I refused to make a sound, much less ask to be taken back. It could've been the last decision I ever made. I didn't care - after all, I was thoroughly brain washed at this point, so even watching my left arm swell to twice its normal size wasn't enough for me to call the Corpsman.

My plan was to pray to pass out from the pain. I'm not kidding. Not a good plan, but it was the best I could come up with at the time. That didn't work, so I was left to writhe around with my skin ON FIRE. The "enemy" did eventually come through. I have no recollection of shooting at them, just the silence afterward, for hours. I came to find out later that our radio had malfunctioned and we weren't able to get the transmission to come back after the firefight.

It was about dawn when we finally came back to camp, and when word got around about what I'd put myself through so as not to kill the mission, I got the begrudging respect I craved from Captain Dye and Gunny.

This was a defining moment for me as an adult, I suppose. An initiation, of sorts, into manhood. Something that I cannot explain happened out there. A switch was flipped. I'm now fully aware how people can risk their lives for reasons that seem ridiculous to others, and I'm no different.

The training continued in the Philippines, and after five months of training and rehearsals, I was more prepared for the shoot than any other I'd ever been a part of. After a fourteen-hour plane ride, we were headed to our hotel in Laoag. During a bus ride to the hotel, Billy Baldwin, who was in the cast and for whom we felt a mutual dislike, informed me they'd given my role to someone else and I'd been downgraded to an extra.

I found out later, this was over what I consider to be a poor table read on my part. I was using a Georgian accent, as my character was supposed to be from Georgia, but the actors playing his wife and father were all using Texan accents instead. Oliver could've directed me to use any accent from virtually any town in Texas and I could've done it, being from there. But instead I lost what I'd hoped would be my "breakthrough" role for trying to make the guy sound authentic.

Have I mentioned it's a brutal business yet? Not as hard as riding BMX professionally, but still...

How Billy Baldwin knew my fate before I did, I never discovered, but I decided to stay on as one of the faceless troops anyway. I could've walked with pay right then and there. But I was in it for my good Captain Dye at that point. The movie took a backseat in my mind.

The first hotel we stayed at was a palatial brick structure on a beautiful beach along the South China Sea. It had been built for the wedding of one of Marcos' daughters, and closed ever since.

They reopened it for us, and there we were in this four-star residence surrounded with ocean, jungle and squalor. It was one of the richest countries in natural resources I'd ever seen, however, Marcos had done such a number on raping the citizens of billions, they might never recover. Bad leaders can do that.

One evening Dye, Tom Sizemore, some of the reserve Marines working on the movie, and I had planned to take a "fact finding" tour of the local Red Light District. We were all set to leave when we heard the gunfire of rebel insurgents in the distance.

I asked Dye if he still wanted to go. His reply, "Commies have been trying to kill me my whole life" gave me some solace, I'm not sure why, and off we went.

Bill Allen

Much like the guy who buys *Playboy* for the articles, I went just to see what was out there. (You know, like a sociologist! Swear!)

Far too nervous to go to a pro and afraid of contracting God knows what deadly disease, I ended up merely chatting with a young prostitute whose parents owned the brothel. She was paying for her siblings to go to school, and she saw nothing taboo, illicit or wrong with her life, so I certainly didn't judge her. In fact, being an actor, we probably had more in common than I realized.

We also stayed in Manila for some time in a four-star hotel, while all around was dire poverty. It was poverty on a scale we haven't seen in this country since the depression. I remember people choking the sidewalks, selling everything from pencils to themselves. Yet, as I have found in other poverty-stricken, non-Westernized cultures, even in such deplorable circumstances, the people had a happier outlook than the vast majority of Americans I know. It seems to stem from closer family units and self-reliance.

The shooting went as expected—hot, humid, and with zero glamour. We had to stay in character as Marines between takes. After being well preconditioned all that time in marine training, the line between fantasy and reality blurred. As I said, it had long before become something more than a movie - it was a fully immersive experience along the lines of *Tropic Thunder*, which I'm convinced was inspired by one of Oliver's productions.

My RAD Career

I was the grenadier in our unit and I had attached to my M-14 a non-explosive yet still very lethal dummy grenade that I happened to be a dead shot with. By the time filming rolled around, I felt like Private Pyle in *Full Metal Jacket* and had transferred all of my hate from the army of North Vietnam onto...? Oliver, for recasting my role without telling me, when I could have so easily satisfied his concerns and kept the part.

I spent most of my days on set musing about how easy it would be to put that grenade right between Ollie's running lamps and make it look like an accident.

I figure I would've gotten an ovation from the entire cast and crew. I used to wonder why I didn't do it, considering my state of mind at the time. It was always missed opportunities and crushed dreams with Oliver, but I still get residual checks to this day.

After arriving home I became pretty dejected over the whole *Born on the Fourth* experience and was still stinging over it when Brandon decided to cheer me up by taking me camping in one of his favorite spots in the Sierra Nevadas.

Little did we know what weirdness awaited us...

CHAPTER FIFTEEN

It took us driving several hours to get to the scenic mountain town of Bishop. We came loaded for bear, literally. Brandon, an experienced outdoorsman, made sure we were well equipped for going deep into the mountains for a couple of weeks. I brought everything except for a sleep pad (a Marine doesn't need no stinking sleep pad, turns out *I* did) including my M1 rifle and enough ammo to stave off an army of fed up bears.

With my impeccable driving skills, we pulled into the trailhead parking lot and I drove off the edge, leaving my front wheels spinning in the air. Figuring it was a good theft deterrent we left it that way and started an uphill climb that would last a couple of days.

Since leaving civilization, Brandon had taken on a countenance I hadn't seen before. He was quiet, undemonstrative, and completely in his element. As I said, he'd been thrown out of Catholic high school for spitting up the holy sacrament, but here he found reverence.

He mentioned he'd once seriously considered being a mountain man for real, but with a Zen delivery told me, "I have things to do first."

It had been days since we'd seen another human being. Before I realized it, we were well beyond help if anything went seriously wrong. But that didn't enter my mind until we were so high up the steep mountain there wasn't even a good place to pitch a tent.

With the sun dropping fast, we were able to find the only suitable area for camping on the mountain, or so it looked to me. The vantage point was breathtaking, however, and we made camp and ate just as the sun gave way to night.

Brandon unexpectedly pulled out a small piece of paper with some repeated drawings. Blotter acid. Oh, God. He acted surprised when I was more than willing to play his reindeer games. We ate two hits apiece and settled in for the ride of a lifetime.

I hadn't done any hallucinogens since high school but this was clearly different than anything I'd ever done back then, much more dramatic, and considering the setting, much more dangerous.

Early in the evening, while chatting in the tent, Brandon announced that at one point, he'd have to leave the tent.

This filled me with a terror that took me by surprise. I chose to try to prevent him from leaving, hoping he'd forget—a thought that proved I was losing my grip. We started discussing Mike Vendrell, Brandon's Sensei, and his reported abilities to dematerialize and walk through walls, among other things.

The wind started to rock the tent, and it looked as if it was being hit by colored lights from the outside. It was then that Brandon announced, "I gotta go" and before I had the chance to freak out, he was out the flap and G-O-N-E.

I didn't want to be in there alone, so I jumped out after him. BAD IDEA. The second I got my bearings outside, I witnessed something I will never forget, real or imagined. The wind started kicking up wildly as the full moon leapt from behind the mountains in an instant. One second it wasn't there, and then BANG, it lit up the sky and mountain range like a fireworks display. This was shocking enough to knock me on my ass, which it did.

Then things started to get really interesting...

The clouds, like something out of one of Tim Burton's nightmares, started forming into ghostly images of skeletons and disembodied spirits. I grabbed the rock I sat on and noticed it had taken on a molten look. The entire mountain range itself pulsated with life. This shocked me into action, which was to scream for Brandon. I got no reply. The wind was blowing so hard anyway, he probably couldn't have heard me if he was sitting beside me.

Which. He. Wasn't.

I decided to go get my rifle in the tent before I went for Brandon, as if that would do me any good, and jumped back inside.

As soon as I did, Brandon suddenly appeared back in the tent and closed the flap. This had the effect of putting the lid back on Pandora's Box. Everything got eerily quiet and I immediately felt better.

We discussed what we'd each seen. Brandon said he went outside and lay down and when he opened his eyes, he was in a graveyard. A prophetic vision in retrospect, however, if I'd had the insight to understand, nothing would've changed. Amazingly, I had told Brandon earlier in the evening that I feared for his early demise - not because of any special psychic abilities I had or anything, but because he was such a wild man.

I told him, "My brother was number one, Kirk was number two, I think you'll be number three."

Brandon replied by saying, "Don't talk that way..." which was surprising, given that he'd told me many times he felt he was "racing the clock," a sentiment his father had also expressed.

It was a few hours before I got the courage to poke my head outside the tent, and I needed confirmation for what I saw when I finally did.

"Brandon, you'd better see this."

Brandon stuck his head out, and what unfolded next was truly sublime. The clouds started charging over the mountain range, projecting an image of a nude woman. Her belly grew as she passed overhead. Inverted in her stomach, was the unmistakable outline of a fetus, ready to come out.

I gasped, and whatever we saw, it was the same thing at the same time. I was again shocked at the beauty and immediacy of the "vision" and Brandon's nonchalant attitude. We retreated back into the tent, and after Brandon passed out, I packed up our things TO GET OFF THAT MOUNTAIN.

I'd had the crap scared out of me and thought that being back in civilization would help. It didn't. Only time helped bring me back to reality, but even then an acute awareness of what was lurking at the edge of waking life can ruin your breakfast.

We got off the mountain after only two nights with the help of a kindly park ranger named Herb. Herb then became the nickname we had for God or "otherness." Brandon commemorated our trip on a T-shirt I still own that say's "Goethe Lake, 10,900' Thanks Herb." Otherwise I might think I dreamt the whole thing.

Brandon's career exploded right after this trip, and I kept playing with the band and getting acting jobs here and there. It was a good time, watching the friends I'd come along with start to slay some dragons.

CHAPTER SIXTEEN

I was living with Brandon in a small servant's cottage he rented in the Hollywood foothills that was part of a large gated house and pool compound. I should've known something was coming. One day, after he'd already starred in *Rapid Fire* and *Showdown in Little Tokyo* he threw a script he was reading at me and said, "This is great. They kill me in this one."

The title of the script was *The Crow*. I'm not a comic book guy, so had no awareness of the graphic novel, and was a bit turned off by the brutal violence. This was one of the things that Brandon found fascinating and before long he was spending six hours a day at the gym in preparation for the role.

I was used to him taking off for a couple of months at a time to go on location. So when he said he was leaving for North Carolina I didn't think much of it. We were to see each other in Mexico right after the shoot, where he and his girlfriend of two years, Eliza, were getting married.

We talked a couple of times during production, but he was working endless days, and I tried not to bother him. On the evening of March 30th, 1993, I got a call from Carol saying that she'd heard through Eliza that Brandon had been injured on the set, and she was flying out to see him.

I immediately told Lou about the accident. He'd recently been dragged almost to death by a runaway horse while filming *Young Guns 2* and knew the value of waking up to a kind face in the hospital, so he suggested I get my ass out there and even offered to pay, so I booked the next flight out.

My itinerary had me stopping at more than one connecting airport. Somewhere in the Midwest I was coming out of the airport restroom, when three federal agents stopped me, addressed me by name, and asked where I was headed.

I said a friend had been injured on a movie set and I was going to see him. One of the agents had read about Brandon on the wire, so corroborated my story. It was only then that they told me why I was stopped. Apparently a red flag went up when I booked a one-way ticket and immediately got on a plane. I think they thought I was pedaling drugs or something.

They wished me luck and left. I was amazed. You have to figure people booking last-minute travel arrangements and showing up for said arrangements happens a lot, but they had three Feds on it.

This incident played in my mind many times after 9/11 and hearing the stories of the hijackers being reported by their flight instructors to the FAA because they hadn't been interested in learning to land planes, only to take off and maneuver. Where were the Feds then? And what about when they were listed as being known terrorists?

A driver for the movie company picked me up in Wilmington. We made small talk, but instead of taking me to the hospital as I'd expected, she pulled up in front of the house Brandon was renting. I got out and Brandon's stunt double, Jeff Cadiente, looking remarkably like Brandon, asked me if I'd heard.

"Heard what?"

"He didn't make it."

I could not believe my ears. Of course I lost it, in front of God and everybody. I wasn't able to sit with my grief but for a few seconds before I was told Brandon's fiancée was in the house, having just found out herself. I went in and sat with Eliza who was inconsolable. After a couple of minutes we got more bad news...

Brandon's mother, sister, and step-dad were landing soon, and we were to go meet them and tell them Brandon was dead. I flashed to being thirteen years old when I happened to be the only person home with my mother when the cops came to the house and told us my older brother had died in a skiing accident.

My mother's grief was more than I was capable of handling at the time. This was a scene I'd never want to be a part of again, yet here I was, a principal player. Eliza and I were whisked to the airport to do the deed. Had we been thinking more clearly, we'd have had the driver pick up the family inside the terminal and play dumb like she'd done with me.

No, Eliza and I went inside and waited for the commuter plane to disembark. We held each other and watched in horror as we saw the family on the tarmac, laughing and smiling, completely unprepared for what was to come. They'd visited Brandon in the hospital many times before, so I'm sure they thought this injury was one he'd walk away from, too.

Of course, as soon as they got inside and saw us, no words were needed. They could read our faces and there was no use denying what had happened. Remember the last episode of *The Mary Tyler Moore Show* when everyone in the office was in a tearful group hug and they all moved collectively to get some Kleenex? That's what we looked like, a beast with ten legs, crying and shuffling through the terminal as one.

Brandon had three memorials - one for business associates held at his manager's house in Beverly Hills, one for his friends at Lou's house, and a small funeral and burial in Seattle.

The funeral was one for the books. I flew straight to Seattle from North Carolina, so this was the first time I got to see my L.A. friends, Carol, Miguel, Steve Lukather, and Louis Abernathy, a director and writer. It was a much-needed reunion, as I needed to see some familiar faces. However, things were about to get weirder than they already were.

Miguel informed me that Vendrell would soon be arriving and that he'd already seen Brandon on the "other side." The story, as Miguel told it, was that when it was announced that Brandon was hurt on the radio, Mike had been driving and he pulled over to the side of the road and immediately jumped out of his body via astral projection (a conscious separation of body and spirit with the ability to return to the body).

He quickly found Brandon, still attached to his body by a thin silver cord. Brandon was giddy and begged Mike to come with him. Mike tried to coax Brandon back into his body instead. Brandon said that he was mind, spirit and body, and he had no idea what his body would be like when he returned and didn't want to find out. He'd always wanted to be in "the Twenty-Seven Club" anyway (a term used to refer to Jimi Hendrix, Jim Morrison, and Janis Joplin who all died at that fateful age) even though he'd turned twenty-eight the day *The Crow* started filming.

"I'm a God, Mike."

"No, you're not, Brandon."

Brandon snapped the delicate silver cord.

"I am now."

Mike summoned Leong, his disembodied spirit guide and Sensei, and after the traditional martial arts bow, Mike and Brandon parted, and Leong accompanied Brandon to the light.

Suffice it to say that I wanted to see Mike as soon as he got in so he could tell me about it all himself, and possibly put me in touch with Brandon. I found him once he landed, and he was upbeat as usual. I was still too stunned to even notice.

I said that I'd heard that he'd been in touch with Brandon. He told me his version of the amazing events and explained that he'd called on Leong because he didn't trust Brandon to go into the light by himself, fearing he might've gone to the dark side first.

"You know Brandon."

Indeed.

I asked him if he could contact Brandon for me.

He said that he'd try sometime later, and he'd let me know.

I went to dinner with the L.A. gang. We were somehow able to find some humor, just to stave off the pain. I shared that I felt bad that I wasn't able to fulfill Brandon's last wishes, that when he died he wanted to be cooked up and eaten in a stew by his friends.

When Louis heard this he said he'd been a private eye at one time and could get into any lock in the country, alarm or not, and that if Brandon was *his* best friend he'd do it. I was left with a decision that would haunt me for the rest of my life.

The day of the funeral came and I was given the unfortunate duty of getting everyone into the limos and being head pallbearer. I walked outside the hotel to find Vendrell out in the rain pacing back and forth, rubbing his palms together and looking up at the sky. I asked what he was doing.

"Stopping the rain for the funeral," he said, matter-of-factly.

I was a little too preoccupied with my duties to take much note. We all settled into the limos, and in a few minutes pulled past the throngs of photographers lining the gates of Lake View Cemetery. It was only when I got out of the car that I realized the rain stopped as soon as we arrived. The sun seemed to come out right above the small gathering beside Brandon's coffin, about to be laid to rest beside his father's grave.

I found Mike and said, incredulously, "Hey, it stopped raining." He gave me a look that said he was surprised at my surprise.

The service was performed by Brandon's mother, Linda, in the same spot where she'd buried Bruce twenty years before. Brandon had just taken me to this same place the previous year to introduce me to his dad.

The air was thick with grief, although I do remember Miguel having me nearly pissing my pants, laughing over some cynical observation, a thing Brandon would've wholly approved of.

After the service, the mourners were filing to the limos when Mike came up to me.

"C'mere Slim, the juice is pretty strong right now."

He led me to the gaping hole that contained our dear friend. I sat down on a plastic folding chair, overlooking the open grave. Mike moved behind me and started rubbing his hands together and told me he didn't know how long he could hold "it," whatever "it" was. He then placed his hands on my head and ... nothing. No fireworks, my head didn't explode, just silence.

Then I heard it.

"SLIM, I'M RIGHT HERE, SLIIIIIIIIIIM!!!"

It was Brandon, loud and clear.

Mike dropped his hands and apologized for not being able to hold the energy. I wept like a child at the realization that Brandon's spirit was still very much alive, and I was still loved through the veil of tears.

Days later, Miguel and I stayed up the night before the memorial held at his manager's, Jan McCormack's house, drinking and putting together a tape of Brandon's favorite tunes to play during the gathering. Of course, I forgot to bring the tape the next day, only to quickly regret it as I passed the throngs of hustlers in their Armani suits into Jan's house and heard Whitney Houston's "I Will Always Love You" over the speakers. Brandon would've thrown up.

I had to hold it in. I don't remember much about the affair, I suppose it's because most of the people there barely knew Brandon. Melissa Etheridge was kind enough to show up and sing a tune. I gave a talk and somehow managed to not pass out.

Upon leaving, I saw Stephen Segal talking to reporters, saying that if Brandon's death was a criminal act and he was going to get to the bottom of it since he was an old friend of the family (total BS). Wow, I couldn't believe the balls on that guy. I'd seen him only once before (as had Brandon!) when we'd visited the set of *Out For Justice* and he'd lied to Brandon then about knowing his father and appeared to be pretty full of himself.

In the movie there was a stunt that involved Segal rolling over a saloon bar, and he was supposed to knock over some bottles as he did it. After he blew several takes, the director practically begged him to knock over the bottles as he rolled over the bar, and a grizzled prop guy yelled out, "Burt Reynolds woulda done it!"

This gave us all an opportunity to laugh at Stephen. The next take the bottles went over.

Stephen's presence at the memorial seemed emblematic of a bunch of the people there in that they weren't Brandon's friends, yet there they were mourning a guy they hardly knew. It felt wrong.

The next memorial, held at Lou's house, was special as it was attended only by Brandon's friends, including the old poker crowd, and if Brandon was watching I'm sure he loved it. The mourners were encouraged to eat a bowl of "Brandon Stew" cooking on the stove, while vegetarians were required to eat two.

I found a recording to start of the festivities: the Monty Python song, "I Like Chinese."

Bill Allen

"I like Chinese, I like Chinese,
They only come up to your knees,
They're cute and cuddly, and ready to please.
I like Chinese food, the waiters never are rude..."

This made everyone uneasy, another move Brandon would've fully enjoyed. Even Miguel, who has an enormously rude sense of humor, was uncomfortable with the choice and begged that it stop.

Then Melissa got up and sang Pink Floyd's "Wish You Were Here" and brought the place to a screeching halt. Lou finished off the event by reading Brandon's favorite poem, "The Raven," which Brandon knew by heart and read aloud in *The Crow*. (Sigh...). I saw him recite it once at his family cabin in the mountains outside of Los Angeles, tripping and shirtless, giving the performance of a lifetime.

Brandon's accidental early demise traumatized me so completely; I was no longer excited by acting or being on a movie set. It took all the glitter out of Tinseltown for me, and I bumped around L.A. for the next couple of years kinda lost. Carol and I broke up and I moved in with my vocal coach, Leslie.

Several months after Brandon's death, I was at Leon's house and met a lovely young actress who Leslie and I had a great time talking to, Toni

DeRose, a regular on NBC's *Providence* and *Murder One*.

We soon became very close friends, but I had no idea at the time she would become more than an acquaintance. Toni soon revealed to us something she normally kept secret. In fact, she hadn't told anyone in her life except her best friend, but for some reason she felt compelled to tell us that she had the ability to talk to the dead through automatic writing. (This is the ability to have spirits channel their thoughts through her hand while she writes. Sounds nuts, I know...)

This got my attention as I was still heavily grieving for Brandon. I asked her if she'd be willing to do a session with me.

A couple of days later I called Toni and she mentioned that she and Brandon had been practicing - that is, he'd been practicing writing with Toni's hand. I found this a bit unsettling but headed over with an open mind.

I was driving my Datsun 1600, an old car of his that Brandon had given me shortly before he died. A two-seater convertible, it was a rust bucket that I was in the middle of restoring when he passed. Brandon never got to see it in its beautiful, completed condition. I was so proud of that car, and I wished every day he'd been able to see how well it turned out. It made me feel a bit closer to him to drive it around.

I arrived at Toni's and she was pleased to see me and assured me that Brandon was already there. She told me that she would do a protective prayer, and that the temperature in the room would likely drop a few degrees. She asked her spirit guides to bless this session and to let Brandon "through." As foretold, the room suddenly became cooler, and a presence seemed to fill the space. Toni started scribbling on a legal pad, pen in hand, making wild, unintelligible strokes and whispering to herself. The first thing I understood was when she spoke up and asked,

"How's the car?"

I felt as if my heart was ripped out of my chest. I hadn't told Toni *anything* about the Datsun. I wept almost immediately. "Brandon" and I got to chat about some personal issues that were left unresolved when he died, and it gave me the feeling of closure. Amazing as it may seem, I had no doubt after that first question that I was talking to him. His personality was as individual and strong as it was when he was alive, so I considered this a rare opportunity.

Toni facilitated contact between Brandon and me through several sessions after that, and I felt healed to the point that I felt I could let him go to do his work, whatever that was.

I found my sessions with Toni to be utterly remarkable, and incredibly healing. It opened my mind to even more possibilities than I'd considered before. The last session I had proved to be the most dramatic.

Again I was at Toni's and chatting with Brandon through her hand. I don't recall the subject, I don't think it was too earth shattering. I thought the chat was about to end when Brandon unexpectedly asked, "Slim, do you want to talk to my Dad?"

"Sure."

I could barely comprehend what was about to happen. A very solemn energy entered our space.

"Hello, Slim."

"Hello, Bruce."

The conversation was brief but dramatic. And then I asked simply if he and I had any sort of connection.

His answer was beautiful.

"Only as loving supporters of earthly Brandon."

This hit me like a bullet between the eyes. And then...

Toni held out her hand (or rather, Bruce *used* Toni's hand) to shake mine. I held mine out as well, and shook Toni/Bruce's hand, and then he was gone as quickly as he arrived.

CHAPTER SEVENTEEN

Toni and her gift came to the rescue many times, but a conversation we had after these others provided the most compelling evidence yet that she was not coming up with these stories on her own, or delusional. I didn't need any more evidence after that first session, but it was still fun when *this* happened...

I'd made plans to go visit her. She was a busy actress, and it was rare that she was available.

I got into the Datsun, which we now called "the Crow Car," and I couldn't get it in gear no matter what I tried. I called Toni and told her that it wouldn't be possible for me to come over that day. Toni then asked if she should have her grandfather, Peter, get his mechanic to look at the Crow Car.

I had come to learn during our automatic writing sessions that Peter was her dead grandfather, Peter DeRose, a famous Tin Pan Alley songwriter who penned the jazz standard, "Deep Purple." And now in the afterlife he was an archangel and Toni's spirit guide. Yes, I know how it sounds.

So when she asked if Peter's mechanic should look at the car, I immediately understood that she meant her "dead" grandfather's "dead" mechanic. I had a bit of trouble grokking the situation, but I agreed, and she told me to call back in a few minutes.

When I did, she said something that floored me.

"Well, his mechanic looked at the car and there's nothing wrong with it. He said there's a leak in the slave seal, but the car is okay to drive."

It had been six weeks or so since my Datsun mechanic, forty minutes away in El Monte, had told me with confidence that, "the car is fine to drive but it has a leak in the (wait for it...) slave seal."

To this day, I have no idea what the hell a slave seal is, just that you can drive a car with a leaky one. I thanked Toni, went down to my carport, and realized the shifter handle had come unscrewed. I screwed it into place, started up and headed to Toni's.

Before I knew it, my girlfriend Leslie and I met some folks starting a spiritual community in New Mexico headed by a Native American medicine singer, Thomas One Wolf, and we moved to Northern New Mexico.

It was a rash decision but I needed to get a break from Hollywood, as there were now ghosts on every street corner, from Brandon to Carol, who I still carried a torch for.

Bill Allen

Tres Piedras is one of those hole-in-the-road towns that when most people drive through, they shake their heads and wonder, "Who the hell lives here?"

That seemed perfect to me. Several of us bought into a 2,500 acre plot and were given stewardship over five acres apiece.

I brought an Airstream trailer from North Carolina and jackknifed the pickup and trailer on a Tennessee highway late one night. Fun. I somehow survived, and we pulled it into perfect desolation in the middle of a sage-filled pinion pine forest, surrounded by mountains as far as the eye could see. We built and attached a mudroom, and pulled the plug on the "out world," as Thomas called it. Weekly sweat lodge ceremonies became our church, and these were some of the richest times of my life.

I'd always said I wanted to learn to build houses one day, and in New Mexico I did just that. I learned construction by building people's houses on the land, mostly Californians who would only visit occasionally, including David Faustino of *Married with Children,* and his brother, Michael. There were at least twenty or so of us that lived on the land fulltime in everything from tents and lean-to's to fully functioning houses, all off the grid.

This is a harsh place to carve out a living, and a harsher place to live. At an elevation of over 8,000 thousand feet, the winters can reach thirty below zero. The closest town, Taos, is a forty-minute drive each way, if you needed a nail or a hospital, or both.

The unexpected thing I came to discover in New Mexico is that it has a thriving film industry, and soon I was auditioning and working in New Mexico as an actor. Eventually I started working more as an actor there than I had in L.A. for some time, and the competition all had regular lives, so the atmosphere in casting sessions was infinitely friendlier.

I'd only been in New Mexico for a couple of years when I got a job on a cable series called *Lazarus Man*, starring Robert Urich. His resume included starring in dozens of TV series, and ol' Rob seemed completely over it. Too much time in a movie star trailer had taken its toll. He was in a position that most actors would walk over their grandmother's grave for, and he appeared miserable. So when he contacted cancer soon after the series ended, I could not have been less surprised.

After my first day of working on *Lazarus*, I got the call sheet with next day's shooting schedule.

I looked to see who the guest stars were. The first was Max Gail, of *Barney Miller* fame, whom I'd met years before when Lou took me to his house for my first Indian sweat lodge ceremony that put me on the "red road" (following Indian spiritual paths), eventually leading me to New Mexico.

The next name was familiar but not immediately recognizable to me, Michael Massey. My body began shaking before it registered. This was the actor who'd shot and killed Brandon on the set of *The Crow*. I wasn't sure how to react. This was too much. I thought I'd moved a thousand miles away to avoid being repeatedly reminded of Brandon's death, and here it was staring me in the face.

I immediately called Thomas One Wolf and shared my predicament. I'd already decided that if the tables were turned and Brandon had come across the guy who'd put a bullet in my gut, he'd at least sucker punch him. Thomas assured me that Michael was a victim of the incident as much as Brandon. This helped somewhat, but I knew I had to meet Michael anyway.

The coincidence that Max, who'd played a key role in my spiritual awakening, and Brandon's killer and I were all on a random TV show set on the same day in the middle of nowhere, far away from the locations of either event did not escape me, and I was prepared for the outcome.

Michael was on the schedule to begin filming in the morning, and I wasn't due on set until after lunch, so I made it a point to show up while he was still there. To my dismay, I arrived just in time to witness Michael playing another bad guy and trying to twirl his six-shooter and not doing a very good job of it, fumbling and almost dropping the damn thing. I can understand that he didn't want to play with guns after Brandon's death, but here he was again trying to pull off a maneuver with a gun that he was not qualified for.

I won't go into the whole story of how Brandon got killed, but the final fatal error in a string of many, was Michael needlessly pointing the loaded firearm directly at him instead of cheating off to the side as an actor is supposed to do on set.

I made my way over to Michael and introduced myself as Brandon's best friend. He didn't act surprised. He said he was sorry. It obviously came out wrong, but I said I wasn't sorry (that Brandon was my best friend). I took a deep breath, remembering what Thomas had said, and told him that I forgave him for what happened.

He said that I was the first person from Brandon's camp to let him off the hook in any fashion. We ended up having lunch together along with Max. The enormity of the situation was staggering, but necessary for healing.

There was another ghost I had a hard time shaking... Carol's sister had moved with her family out to New Mexico when I told them about the community.

Because of this, I would occasionally see Carol when she came to visit. This was somewhat uncomfortable while Leslie and I were living together. But as time wore on, Leslie became more of a sister, and my thoughts constantly turned to Carol. She visited once while Leslie was out of town and I declared my love for her. Carol had long since gotten over me with a lot of help and coaching, but I could see that we still might have a future. I shared the uncomfortable truth with Les, and we tearfully parted ways.

Carol and I began a long-distance relationship, seeing each other over the next five months, and rediscovering the love that was there all along.

That spring we planned to go to New York to see Lou perform in *The King and I* on Broadway. After a meal at a Chinese restaurant in SoHo on our last night, I opened a fortune cookie that read, "Will you marry me, sweet William?" As my jaw hit the floor, "Wedding Bell Blues" came over the sound system. ("Bill, I love you so, I always will...")

I looked up to see the whole restaurant looking at me expectantly, the waitress and hostess with tears in their eyes. Of course I said yes. How could I ruin Carol's special moment? It had been my wish early on to marry her and it's easily the best decision I've ever made. And having seen so many close to me choose the wrong mate and knowing that is the single worst decision anyone can make, I feel like the luckiest man alive.

She moved out and joined me in my fabulous Airstream and fought the good fight in the boonies of New Mexico. Even after finding Leslie's tampons in the trailer, she stayed with me. Soon after she came out, the community ran into legal troubles with the county, and we were no longer allowed to do any construction on the land. Thankfully, this was not before I'd built a cute little adobe cottage for my mother's retirement.

Soon New Mexico reversed their tax breaks and other financial incentives for film and television projects, causing all the acting jobs to dry up, too. Carol and I were left to clean up rental properties in the Taos ski valley and to sell pottery in a gift shop for a whopping $7 an hour, wondering how long we could last. After about a year of this Carol came to me and said, "I'm going back to California, you comin' with me?"

My bags were packed in a matter of minutes.

Bill Allen

CHAPTER EIGHTEEN

Arriving back in L.A. after five years in the wilderness was a bit of a culture shock. I was still a mountain man in many respects and it took months, if not years to re-acclimate. I suppose peeing indoors was the biggest adjustment and dealing with our neighbors at the time who were, ahem, female professional um...WHORES!!

After living in a spirit-based community, where most of us lived a monk-like existence, Carol and I shared a duplex deep in the San Fernando Valley with some working girls and their boyfriend escort. All night parties were a regular occurrence next door. Since my wife would've frowned upon me boring a glory hole through our adjoining wall, my "neighb-whores" were of no use to me.

I spent the first few years back in L.A. working as a handyman as Carol grew her astrology practice. Acting in L.A. proved difficult for a middle-aged guy who took a big time out and then tried to resurrect his career, and the demands of the handyman job were enough to keep me from focusing on it much anyway. I did a couple of plays during this period, just to keep my hand in it. Most of my acting roles over the years have still come out of New Mexico (where they wisely reinstated those financial incentives for film and TV production). I kept my ties strong with the "Land of Entrapment" because my Mom still lived there.

As a result I've been blessed to work with some amazing talent and on at least one iconic TV show, *Breaking Bad,* with the great Bryan Cranston (the funniest guy ever). I did some movies with some other talented souls including Billy Bob Thornton (*Astronaut Farmer* - I play Reporter #3. Don't blink!); Natalie Portman, Jake Gyllenhaal, Toby Maguire, and James Sheridan (*Brothers* - I play a cop and have a few lines); Renee Zellweger (*My One and Only* - yup, that's my voice in the voiceover as you see a close-up of my thumb holding her foot. I got to hold her foot for a full day, actually. A sweeter movie star I've never met. Ahhh...), and Michael Perrineau (*Felon* - I got to pull out all the stops on this one, and cried from six camera angles for six hours, while essentially begging for my life. Michael would make you cry like a little girl, too. Chilling.).

Soon after moving back to L.A., Carol and I moved yet again and spent a year-and-a-half in northern California where we took care of her dying father and settled his affairs. We returned with a generous windfall of insurance money from Al's estate so were able to put a down payment on a lovely cottage in a very Norman Rockwell-esque part of town where we still live.

Bill Allen

Music continues to be a big part of my life. I just wrapped up a three-and-a-half year stint as part of the house band for a famous blues jam at the Pig 'N Whistle in Hollywood. This was an opportunity to play and hang with some of my musical heroes including Kenny Wayne Shepherd, Steve Lukather, Chuck Kavooras, Sugar Ray Rayford, Lance Lopez, Bugs Henderson, not to mention my brother, Sherman, and so many more.

Bugs was a childhood guitar hero of Sherman and mine from Texas. He was my favorite of the local blues giants including Stevie Ray Vaughn and Freddie King. We became dear friends after I moved to California, and he was instrumental in helping me to rekindle my relationship with my brother, Sherman, after years of estrangement. I would see Bugs when he came out and even booked a couple of gigs for him through the old Pipefitters promoter. One such gig had to be shut down due to the lack of a liquor license, and many of my friends ended up in handcuffs, including Brandon. That was fun.

We lost Bugs in 2011 to cancer, so as a tribute Sherman and I produced a CD of Bugs' music with Chuck Kavooras, owner of SlideAway Studios. This has proven to be the most rewarding musical endeavor of my life and I'm honored to be playing on Ray Wylie Hubbard's and Lou Diamond Phillips' tracks. The record is called *The King of Clubs* and includes performances by Lou, Lukather, Orianthi (the amazing female guitarist from the ill-fated Michael Jackson *This Is It* tour and movie), Kenny Aronoff, Paul Reed Smith, Sugar Ray Rayford, and some of L.A.'s best studio musicians. We can't believe how well it came out. You can find it here: https://storecdbabyc.om/cd/

bugshendersontributecd

CHAPTER NINETEEN

As the years have passed, *RAD* and its impact has become more and more clear to me. It took the release of the VHS for the film to catch fire.

It was in the top ten home video rentals for two years, and as those around at the time can attest (re: this long-lost technology), the tapes get worn out from multiple viewings. Videos weren't cheap - they retailed for around a hundred bucks. So most kids would drive their mothers mental by making them "step to" and get it rented for the millionth time until many simply reported it lost and kept it, playing it 'til it was a pile of dust.

Even though bootleg DVD copies are easily obtained, these VHS tapes are treasured to this day. I've seen copies still in shrink wrap go for $1,000.00. It was in the ensuing years when I was off doing other acting jobs and getting involved in music while almost never thinking of the film that it was creeping into the DNA of rabid fans. I would occasionally get recognized in public and if this happened in front of my wife I was generally in for some extra lovin' later on. So that was cool but reconnecting with fans was a gradual process. I slowly began to realize the impact that *RAD* had on so many lives. It still blows me away.

Although I'd receive the occasional fan letter, the first big public display of *RAD* fandom I ever witnessed occurred at a friend's book signing and release party at a swanky restaurant on Melrose Avenue, a trendy section of Hollywood, in 2007. This was one of those red carpet events that I rarely attend, mostly because nobody ever invites me.

We pulled up in my wife's car we lovingly call "the crease mobile" (it got its name when a trash bin "jumped in front of the car" – her words, not mine!). I had no idea there would be photographers and paparazzi.

We pulled straight up to the red carpet, and I yelled, "KEEP GOING, KEEP GOING!!!!" I wanted to park down some side street. But Carol is no shrinking violet. She replied, "No way, Man," and before I knew it, we were greeted with blank stares and no flash bulbs as we exited her "bumper car" and slunk into the establishment.

How do I get myself into these things? The only reason I wanted to go was that I heard the creator of *The Simpsons*, Matt Groening, was going to be there. Matt, however, didn't show but other celebs did, including Amy Brenneman (*Judging Amy*), Paris Hilton's parents, and Coolio (*Coolio?*)...

As we were leaving we ran the gauntlet of paparazzi, stalkarazzi, photographers, autograph hounds, civilians, and press back to the valet so he could pull up in front of everybody in the splendor of our crunched '03 Corolla.

As we stood uncomfortably waiting, one of the autograph hounds turned to me.

"Are you Bill?" he asked.

"Uh, I'm 'a' Bill," I replied, having no idea I'd been "made."

His eyes widened and he said, "Don't go anywhere – be right back!" He went running off and before I knew it, Carol and I were surrounded by all the autograph hounds and photographers, flashing light bulbs, and some civilians mixed in for good measure who were suddenly demanding my attention, signature, and photo, while others looked on agog, having no idea who I was.

Soon the original autograph hound returned, gasping and sweaty, proudly holding an 8x10 glossy *RAD* promotion photo of Bart, Lori, and me that had already been signed by Bart and Lori.

I couldn't believe it—this guy had been carrying this thing around for years in the back of his car, waiting for me to sign it. And the chances that I'd ever actually run into him in a city of sixteen million is ridiculous.

This kind of thing had only happened before this at bike events, and then rarely, but this made me realize the movie still had legs.

Back in '09 I was again reminded of the impact of the movie when the de Silva family got in touch with me. I talked to Chris de Silva first who was holding an event for his late brother, Tim, and

My RAD Career

wanted to know if I'd be a part of it. It seems Tim, who grew up in Ontario, Canada, had been a lifelong *RAD* fan.

The movie introduced him to the sport and, as with so many who saw the film, BMX became an obsession of Tim's, and he actually realized his dream of becoming a pro BMX racer. Everyone who knew Tim loved him and was well aware of his enthusiasm for the film.

Once he became a teen he would vet potential girlfriends by making them watch the movie, and if a young lady wasn't utterly entranced by it, the next thing he'd do was show her the exit.

He was not only a champion of the sport, he was a champion of the local kids. He made every effort to promote the sport in his small hometown. Tim was just twenty when a wealthy landowner afforded him the opportunity to build a BMX track on his property on the outskirts of town, and Tim leapt at the chance.

Tim was working the Bobcat himself and was almost done with the construction of the track when the earthmover flipped over onto Tim, fatally crushing him. So when the family contacted me it was to ask if I'd attend a rally to save the track, since it hadn't been properly permitted and was therefore scheduled to be demolished. I was very moved to be a part of his rally and do a bike ride to raise awareness and get signatures to stop the destruction. Everyone was so grateful that I came, and I was beyond grateful for the chance to help in any way I could.

Bill Allen

I met his siblings, Chris and Jessica and his parents, who treated me with undeserved deference. They were such kind people. Also along for the festivities was the great freestyler Jay Miron, the first to do a double backflip on a bike and a real pioneer of the sport.

Jay is soft-spoken and unassuming, yet has the guts of a gunslinger, never doubt that. He told me from his perspective, how *RAD* has impacted the sport and that people had even told him (straight-faced!) that Cru Jones is still out riding the circuit. It was kinda fun to consider that Cru had reached urban myth status, the kind of B.S. I loved hearing as a kid growing up in Texas, though not quite as good as the story of Rod Stewart getting his stomach pumped.

It wasn't long after that I was invited by Keith Mulligan, a major force in the BMX publicity machine as a photojournalist and editor, to be a presenter at the annual NORA cup awards in Las Vegas. This is the Oscars of freestyle BMX, and used to be combined simultaneously with Interbike, the largest bicycle trade show in the world.

The NORA cup awards are attended by the cream of the BMX freestyle world, and it's a time for old friends to hook up and celebrate another year of not dying while performing the most dangerous stunts possible on a bike. Lest anyone forget that a memorial for lost riders is part of every NORA cup awards show, and I promise that has an indelible impact.

My RAD Career

This time the event was held at the prestigious room, "The Joint," at the Hard Rock Hotel. It's an opportunity for 5,000 of the baddest cats on the planet to throw down. And that night the booze was flowing and no one was feeling any pain after the ceremony.

But again, if you didn't realize the bravery of these riders, the tribute they had for my co-presenter, Stephen Murray, was jaw dropping. Steven was a master of the dirt and seeing how he used to soar twenty to thirty feet in the air while performing gravity-defying flips and midair tail whips was enough to make you think this guy was superhuman. His abilities clearly were, however, his body was not, and when he misjudged a landing back in 2007, he became a quadriplegic in an instant.

He has a family that supports him but seeing him wheeled to the podium in front of his colleagues and fans and witnessing the outpouring of love was an overwhelming experience.

For those not too familiar with the sport, misjudging a landing is all a part of riding, and many times this will end you up in the ER if not the morgue. It's a fact that Mat Hoffman got so tired of going to the ER for stitches, he would stitch himself up with no anesthetic. Please watch his documentary, *The Birth of Big Air,* if you haven't already, and it will give you an idea of what these guys do for a living or for the goof. It's an AMAZING film.

Back to that night at Nora - soon it was my time to be announced, and the M.C. said something like, "You grew up wanting to BE this guy, *and now here he is, Cru Jones!*"

I walked onstage, and the place exploded. I've been in the performing arts for thirty-five years now, and this was the first and only time I've ever received that kind of attention. I realize they were reacting to a character I portrayed and not actually to me, and that Justin Timberlake gets that kind of reaction just for brushing his teeth, but *still*. It was a true "deer in the headlights" moment for me.

I yelled out some jokes I'd written but no one seemed to care, they were too busy being drunk and screaming, which was fine. A good time was had by all, and when Daniel Dhers took top honors that night, it was like an old school rumble but instead of stabbing one another, everyone was tossing beer on everyone else, which made those not completely plowed (about three altogether) act indignant and embarrassed.

Earlier that day I showed up at Interbike at the booth of my friend, Bill Ryan, the owner of Supercross BMX. I brought a handful of 8x10 photos to sign to help his company get a little well-deserved attention, and quickly found out I was the prettiest girl in the room when a line of people formed and circled around the convention center and I signed autographs until my wrist gave out. It seemed I'd signed every personal item they'd ever owned. All the while, the only American Tour De France winner we have left, Greg LeMond, was a

My RAD Career

few booths down barely raising an eyebrow of passersby.

This was not long after the very first Olympics to feature BMX, and soon Bill Ryan brought over Donnie Robinson, the bronze medalist, because he was a diehard *RAD* fan.

I saw Donnie coming from a distance, literally bent over and hyperventilating, getting ready to come over and say hi. He was a bit woozy by the time he got to me and was effusive in his love for the movie and the role it had played in his life. To hear an Olympic champion go on and on about how you inspired them is something I have a hard time with since I've never done a backflip, bike or no bike, in my entire life.

Not long after that, a grown man who had just gotten my autograph and was standing next to me burst into tears. I'd bathed that day so I assume it wasn't my body odor, so I'll give "Cru" credit for his display.

I'm not trying to brag here, I'm just beyond amazed by the adulation, especially all these years later. (Remember – I was a cocky young dreamer, who thought the movie would make me famous when it came out... and virtually nothing happened. The fans literally had to grow up!)

It's not lost on me that there are plenty of actors with long careers who have never had the chance to do anything with such a deep and decades-long, life-changing impact. Playing Cru will most likely be the first thing in my obituary,

Bill Allen

and the respect and camaraderie I get from the athletes and fans has made it more than okay by me.

CHAPTER TWENTY

The person most responsible for giving and keeping *RAD* a presence on the web and helping the legacy survive is Jeremy Moser, a fresh-faced and unbelievably cool guy who contacted me several years ago. He has since become a personal friend.

When we first met Jeremy told me he was a stunt rider in *Rad*. Since he's so much younger than I am, I thought what he was saying was impossible and that he was telling what Mark Twain would term, "a stretcher."

So the next time I actually sat through the movie and watched the credits (okay, it's on a continuous loop, projected on every flat surface in my home, 24/7) there's ol' Jeremy's name listed with the stunt riders.

Can I prove that the Jeremy Moser in the credits is the same guy, who can say? (Okay, it is.) All I know is he loves the movie well enough to ride my coattails to any regional BMX race in the country. That proves his diabolical genius. (All right, usually he's the one who's invited and he pulls some strings to get me free tickets, if you must know!)

Bill Allen

He must be a masochist, on top of being the nicest guy in BMX. It was Jeremy who decided to have a 25th anniversary celebration in Canada, complete with showing the film four times at three locations over three days.

The logistics of coordinating such a multi-day event is mind-numbing, between setting up sponsors, making travel arrangements for those the budget would allow, having press lined up, putting together location tours, etc. Honorable mention goes to Brenda Lieberman and Kurt Alksne, the Underground film festival liaisons, who were instrumental in putting things together. But Jeremy was the hero that weekend and those of us who were there are in his debt.

The first night there were two screenings in Calgary, attended by Hal; producer Robert Levy; writers Sam Bernard and Geoffrey Edwards; riders Eddie Fiola, Martin Arparijo, Beatle Rosecrans, and, of course, Jeremy; actors Jamie Clarke (Luke), Kelly McQuiggin (Foxy), and a few others from the movie. A rad event, indeed.

As soon as the lights went down at the first showing people started lighting up what I'm sure must've been Canadian "Herbal" cigarettes, as they sure weren't smoking tobacco. The audience knew all the lines, when to cheer without being prompted, and there were plenty of laughs, a lot unintentional. (How could you keep a straight face while watching the twins hump the floor in matching spacesuits? And yes, Foxy was in the scene also, but she only seemed to get in the way of these two.)

My RAD Career

Classic stuff for any *RAD* fan, but for the people there, many who'd seen the film dozens if not hundreds of times (probably only on TV screens, not two stories tall like this), to be in the same room with the filmmakers and others who shared an unnatural love for the move made it all the better.

After the credits rolled, Eddie and Martin did an impromptu "Bicycle Boogie" on the tiny stage in front of the screen, not meant for performance of any sort. This was a huge hit and an amazing feat, as the smallness of the stage made doing the tricks exponentially more difficult.

I didn't attend the next screening. The theater had a bar, and I was connecting with the fans that made sure I wasn't thirsty, so "not thirsty" I'm thankful I didn't breathe near an open flame.

The second screening let out and I got to hang with the lady I moved the barrier for in the parade scene. You know, the "he's such a nice boy" lady, and also "Foxy" (Kelly McQuiggin) who actually brought along the purple tiger print catsuit. It would maybe fit on her wrist now. We all signed it and she was a real party to be around.

I also had a cute little gal come up to me, Jen, who immediately dropped her pants and had me sign the *RAD* tattoo on her posterior. How could I turn her down? My wife WOULDN'T WANT me to disappoint my fans, I figured. It wasn't the first *RAD* tattoo I've seen, but I had a hard time taking my eyes off this one for some reason, probably the artwork.

The next day I had the opportunity to travel around with Hal and his lovely wife, Ellen, to different TV and radio interviews. I had just read Hal's book, *Stuntman*, and was afforded the opportunity to ask him about it for hours on end. If you haven't read it, it's one of the most mind-blowing showbiz autobiographies I've read and will keep you riveted until the last page.

It's always interesting to compare the public persona vs. the real personality of someone of legendary status. I can tell you the private Hal is old school polite and always a pleasure to be around.

The next screenings were in Cochran, about a half an hour from Calgary. Again the crowds were enthusiastic and determined. There was a couple who flew all the way from Albania and camped out so they could afford to come, and a family that drove two thousand miles from Alabama. This kind of admiration is what keeps the film on people's lips to this day.

It was in Cochrane that Eddie and Martin led a group of some sixty bicyclists to different shooting locations around the city including the lumberyard, the main drag where the parade was held, the hardware store, and the ice cream parlor where Christian and I shared a cone *AND I MADE OUT WITH LORI LOUGHLIN*. (Did I mention us making out? Better go watch the movie again to make sure.)

While filming *RAD* I got to know Talia's stepson, John, who was closer to my age than Jason. He and his friend, Robert, were fresh out of USC

My RAD Career

film school. John has gone on to become one of the most sought-after cinematographers in Hollywood. He's been the director of photography for Michael Bay, and shot the *Spiderman* movies. But his most jaw-dropping job to date in my book is that of *Seabiscuit*. Having shot a horse racing movie, I can appreciate the difficulty of that job. As I've said, the ins and outs of shooting a stampede is no joke and incredibly dangerous.

After seeing *RAD* several times at the 25th anniversary screenings, I believe Jamie did a much better job than I did, and he had little or no experience in front of a camera. A natural, as they say.

He ended up not getting on the Olympic cross-country skiing team, missing by a few hundredths of a second. But he is now a world class mountaineer and has climbed the highest peaks on all seven continents, and Everest twice. He *is* Team *RAD*, as far as I'm concerned. A motivational speaker by day, I have the feeling that he's one of those people who feel most alive while in the "death zone."

As an ultralight pilot, I understand the impulse, but not the stamina it takes to be a mountaineer on that level. The physical pain and loss of brain cells is well documented and quite horrific. I asked Jamie about the trail of bodies one supposedly encounters while climbing Everest and he related a story about cutting down an unfortunate South African guy who died up there years ago but still clung to the mountainside in a horrific frozen tableau, strung up by his ropes. Jamie took the extra effort (a big deal given that no one has any energy to spare on Everest) to cut the gentleman down from his airborne grave and watched as he plunged to the rocks below and shattered into a million pieces like the porcelain figure he'd become. Heavy stuff up there – I'm happy to watch it on *The National Geographic Channel*.

I've stayed in touch loosely with Bart over the years, and he shared with me a great story. It seems Shaquille O'Neal sought him out at a party to tell him what a big fan he was of *RAD*, yet another example of a world-class athlete being touched by the film.

During the filming of *RAD*, the cast and crew stayed at the international Hotel in Calgary, and I had the chance to stay there again for the 25th anniversary celebration. It held many memories, good and bad. I still knew the floor plan and could get around with my eyes closed. I had to do just that before the filming of the "Bicycle Boogie" scene, thanks to that bad fried chicken, after all.

Speaking of that fateful scene, the "Bicycle Boogie" sequence has been recreated at numerous weddings and in many music videos. There's also a rock band named Cru Jones, not to mention a porn star, and a bike shop in Buenos Aries. So the influence keeps spreading, going on thirty-five years.

I guess my main regret now about the shoot was not getting to keep Cru's Mongoose bike and some of the wardrobe. You don't always think of that kind of thing at the time, but being a gypsy at heart, and a bit of a minimalist, I try to not have too much stuff.

Some of the bloopers that fans love are a part of the charm of the film. The most obvious being when Eddie (as Cru) is going over the logs at the lumber yard, you can see the plywood that's nailed to the logs so he (me!) can actually do it.

Another favorite is when Cru and Christian go riding through the woods in yet another musical montage, and they go sailing into the river after hitting a hidden ramp. When Christian (Pat again) hits the drink, you can see his wig stay on top of the water as he goes under. The wig is hard to ignore, but the movie wouldn't be the same without it. The wig is so prominent in the "Boogie" scene it should have its own billing.

So many people have dissected and analyzed this movie, that there are people who will tell you that Cru didn't actually win Hell Track, that he cheated in the qualifying races, and probably WANTED to take his SATs. Who knows? But the fact that these discussions occur means the movie has some staying power, even to this day.

I would recommend starring in a movie that has a worldwide impact and continues to inspire generations decades after its release. It's cool. I've been awarded too much credit but being the face of *RAD* does carry its responsibilities and I've tried to give back to the fans whenever possible. The look of someone who grew up with the film and finally has the chance to talk to a person connected with it (Cru Jones, even), has made it all worth practically freezing parts of myself clean off in that frozen Ass Slide River.

Bill Allen

CHAPTER TWENTY-ONE

I had planned to write some sort of wrap up but cannot continue without acknowledging the passing of the great Hal Needham.

I would not be writing this book without his involvement in my life and readers wouldn't be interested in my story had we not met, as he gave me the break of a lifetime.

With the round of publicity for the 25th *RAD* anniversary and his publicity tour for his memoir, I got to spend some treasured time with him and his lovely wife Ellen, and he was as cool as ever and still the best storyteller I've ever met.

I must say, for BMX fans who are reading this, his early career was the embodiment of the spirit of BMX even though I don't know if he ever even rode a bike - he was too busy diving out of an airplane without a chute, crashing a car at 300 mph, or jumping from galloping horse to galloping horse in front of a team of horses, pulling a fully loaded covered wagon.

But he understood more than anyone the risks involved in his profession, and his list of broken bones, trips to the ER, and near-death close calls were for him part of the job. He looked death in the face a thousand times by the time it actually arrived, and I know he didn't flinch the final time. That kind of experience shaped everything he did and can't be gained by watching life from the sidelines.

Most folks don't know that Hal's famous horse to horse jump in *Little Big Man* was filmed only hours after he had to put down his own favorite horse when it was badly injured during another stunt. And yet there he was, happily risking his neck, smiling ear to ear in that iconic scene. (Seriously – watch the movie just to see him pull this off!) This, my friends, is true grit. The mold was officially broken when he came along.

The other person I have to thank for allowing me to play Cru, of course, is Talia Shire. I'm eternally grateful to Hal and her for putting me in the center of a storm that continues on, so many years later.

For years I was riddled with guilt towards Talia for missing that darn premiere. But once while touring with The Pipefitters I saw her on an airplane and she greeted me with a huge hug and smile as if I really was her long-lost son, no hint of any animosity or disappointment toward me.

It's been an honor to be a part of *RAD* and to be embraced by the BMX community, and to connect with those the film has touched. The enthusiasm for the movie has only increased, and with the release of the Blue-ray 4K version the popularity has exploded. I've been blessed to be a part of many gatherings all over the states and England, Australia, and New Zealand, usually with Martin and Eddie and other BMX legends (even Gary and Craig Turner of famed GT Bicycles went with us to the UK).

I now consider myself an enthusiastic BMX rider after mastering a few injuries and a couple of tricks under Martin's tutelage (I'm the proud inventor of the "no-footed nut buster"). You can find a bunch of us most every Tuesday at sunset at the Huntington Beach Pier riding with freestylers from around the globe. After all, it's where *RAD* still lives.

There is more in store for *RAD* fans, so stay tuned! And keep striving for your own team *RAD* - I think we have room for one more...

MOVIE STAR LESSONS

These guys rocked my world in a way I can barely express. They taught me things that made me a man and they are the reason you are reading this at all. The emphasis of their "teachings" was on acting but the curriculum encompassed much more, of course. Some of the names you'll recognize, some you won't. I picked up things from these badasses that got me results if not the ability to maintain that mantle of "star." It must've worked on a certain level even though I lacked the vision to maintain that status for long, but no one stays on top of the mountain forever. Being first on a call sheet carries a weight nothing can prepare you for. It's a different kind of stress than not being able to pay the bills, but stress is stress, and sometimes the psyche cannot tell the difference between choking on caviar or shit sandwiches.

Bryan O'Byrne

Bryan was a product of the New York acting scene of the 1950s and student of the famed Stella Adler. This was a time and place that produced our finest actors and directors such as Brando, James

Dean, Marilyn Monroe, Arthur Penn, Elia Kazan, and so many more. Bryan embodied the same clear-eyed approach to the work that was emblematic of that era.

Bryan was the first professional acting teacher I ever had. He was brought out by the movie company to work with me when I got my first starring role at a snot-nosed nineteen years of age. He took me seriously at a point in my life when I didn't yet care about my own future. He didn't have enough time or good enough material to get me very far by the day shooting started, but he hammered home a strong work ethic, and a love of acting for the camera. Bryan gave those to me, free of charge. Chuck Berry once wrote, "Back when I got my head together, I wouldn't walk a block but I'd dance a mile."

The script we were working from was God awful, but Bryan showed me how to use it as a tool to see how to break down a character, find his motivations and personality traits. He was into discovering the micro moments that make up a performance, but it took me a while to be able to string them together in a believable fashion.

As I shared earlier, he discovered Nick Nolte as a college football player and encouraged him to become an actor. So his faith in me gave me confidence that he saw something in me even though I had no clue what I was doing. He showed me how to use my feelings towards another actor to tell me how I should approach them in a scene. By obsessing on annoying or lovable traits in another actor, this gives you the point of view that will work for the characters. If another actor, for instance, is playing a character that yours doesn't like, find something cringe-worthy about that actor you can obsess over. It's helpful to keep a distance with people portraying characters at odds with yours. You don't want to develop a friendship that could hurt your onscreen chemistry. But if your character is supposed to have warm feelings towards a particular character, find things to love about the person portraying them and dwell on those. As Bryan always said, "Use it!"

The thing is to find out everything you can about your character - their circumstances, age, background, desires, motivations, gender, and most of all attitudes. Find a strong point of view and what they want in a particular scene and overall.

Bryan treated all of his acting students as though we were his kids, having lost his actual son to a heart attack years before we met. But we had an extra special bond that I will treasure forever that lasted decades until his death. I could write an entire book on that. Suffice it to say he was funny, caring, shocking, brilliant, and generous with his time. A better mentor I couldn't have found. The last time we saw one another, around 2006, we were having dinner and discussing one of his other students, Christopher McDonald (*Happy Madison, Boardwalk Empire*), and how well his career was going. Without a hint of irony or sarcasm, Bryan looked at me and said, "You're next." This was at a time when I had zero going on and had pretty much given up on showbiz. But again I trusted that he saw in me something that I did not. Today I find myself trying to make his prediction come true, sometimes just because he said so. Words matter. He passed away several years ago, and I still remain grateful. Thanks, Bryan.

Adam Roarke

Adam was another product of the NYC actors' scene of the fifties. His career was white hot in the sixties, working in many biker films of the era which were hugely popular. His biggest mainstream films were *Dirty Mary, Crazy Larry* and *The Stuntman*. He was in with the right filmmakers at the right time but had his career derailed for years due to heavy drinking, which he eventually quit. And I mean *serious* fifth-a-day kind of drinking.

By the time we met, he was picking up the pieces of his career, or what was left of it. He was cast as my alcoholic father in my first movie, *And They're Off*. He got on with Miguel, George, and I like a house on fire and initiated me into showbiz with all the hazing they could possibly fit into six months.

That said, Adam was extremely encouraging on and off set to me, and I craved that kind of approval from the guys who came before me. So when he decided to move to Dallas after the shoot and start an acting class, I was his first student.

It was a class geared towards film acting and much was made of that distinction. There's a lot of drama (pun intended) film and TV actors have to deal with that the average high school or college drama department does nothing to address, so in many instances one has to learn on the fly. Adam provided an atmosphere much like that of a film set and we were given the right tools. This was long before acting classes for film were really ever heard of, and there was certainly nothing else like it in Dallas, let alone all of Texas at the time.

There tended to be about eight students or so. We'd all learn the same simple scene and film them back-to-back. During the second half of the class, we would all sit around and watch the replay and critique each other's performance with Adam leading the discussion. A difficult thing to do at first, but for those with some grit and talent, a great way to learn. And since a lot of actors hate watching themselves, it gave Adam's students a distinct advantage.

Adam would often blow smoke up an actor's ass to prop them up, saying inane things like, "You have a wonderful sense of truth." However, when he'd blow smoke up my ass, I opened those cheeks wide cause I was sure that with me he actually meant it.

It was there that I learned to be comfortable in front of the lens and discovered certain tricks that were specific to film acting. To have a professional film actor and actual movie star show us things that most folks didn't have a language for felt like we were behind the curtain and privy to special knowledge. There are things that good film actors do that are imperceptible to the casual observer. A simple look can convey tons of information, if played correctly. And if your face is gonna be forty feet tall, it's important to not suck.

Some of the things a film actor has to deal with include intrusive boom mics, cameras, crew people, extraneous noise and clatter, rude actors, actors on drugs, demanding directors, directors on drugs, obnoxious producers, producers on drugs, and of course, drugs. All the while you're expected to protect your performance and your sanity. These things you don't learn overnight and the quicker you are up to speed, the better for everyone. The biggest problem is no one tells you how to act *after* the lights are shut off. That is a killer, my friends. It nearly undid Adam and so many others it took to an early grave.

Miguel Ferrer

No one else I've known personally has had such a serious showbiz pedigree as Miguel. First child of five born to Oscar-winner Jose Ferrer and 1950s pop star Rosemary Clooney, Miggy was on TV before he could talk as a featured guest on Edward Murrow's TV show, *See It Now*. Things went downhill from there. Jose soon split the scene and Rosemary was left to raise five kids while battling a serious drug addiction to prescription pills. By the time I met Miguel, Rosemary had fully recovered, and Miguel enjoyed a good relationship with Jose. Young Miguel gave up a lucrative drumming career to follow in his father's footsteps. He once said to me, "Slim, I could parachute naked into any city in the world and would have a drumming gig within a week." It took him some time to finally commit to acting, but boy, did he commit.

What Miguel exuded on and off screen was a sense of danger and unpredictability. He had an axe to grind with the world and did he ever leave a mark.

I was psyched to study under him at the Beverly Hills Playhouse and got a good look at how he worked. He had an explosive approach that arose from his own insane background and life. He dealt in excesses and that became what he was famous for onscreen too.

There's a song by Tom Waits that says, "If I exorcise my devils, well, my angels may leave too." I think this is an apt way to look at Miggy's life. His dark side was a large part of who he was and he used it to pay the rent. But wherever you go, there you are, and in fact his devils only left at the very end. He finally gave up drinking and drugs. He died soon after.

I can best sum Miggy up as saying he had a fierce and deadly funny approach to life. He was a difficult task master and the best cheerleader ever. A compliment from him would make me feel I'd accomplished something beyond words. Because his criticism was as stinging as his praise was uplifting, you pretty much knew where you stood with him at all times.

The effect he had on the industry will never be fully recognized because it's widely unknown. He had his fingerprints all over so many things from behind the scenes, including my career and the career of the then unknown George Clooney and so many others. So I'm in pretty good company as a friend whose talent he encouraged and nurtured. Of course, that list includes a young Brandon Lee who Miggy also loved and helped immeasurably as an artist and man. Until I got to work with my friend George Davis, Miguel was the most exciting performer I'd worked with. Brandon and I were able to watch him up close and take what he gave us in any situation.

One of my favorite Miguel quotes, of which there are many was, "There's a world of difference between a talented amateur and a bottom line professional." It was the recognition that hard work is the way to greatness and raw talent is not nearly enough. Would you get on a plane if the pilot only scored high on the aptitude and reflex tests, but had never actually flown?

Miguel was a highly in demand voice-over artist and narrated countless movie trailers. (Pretty much every one that started with "In a world..." was him.) He even voiced *The Crow* trailer!

We had a falling out toward the end of his life, a regret that I carry still. We did make up, I suppose. But he had a harsh way about him that made it difficult for me to continue a relationship. And my mistakes were huge, so I must take some responsibility. Unfortunately, he treated himself the most harshly. He was on the NBC show *NCIS Los Angeles* for the last nine years of his life. The money was good I'm sure, but his talent was largely squandered playing third fiddle to LL Cool J. Don't sell yourself short, Kids. It never works out.

George Clooney

I got to see George at the absolute beginning of his acting career, and as with some of the future big stars I've met, he gave off no indication that he would become what he became - in his case one of the most successful actors of his generation. Make that *ever*.

I attribute a lot of his success to his famous father, Nick, who with his popular Cincinnati talk show gave young George an insider's view of fame and how to handle it. Fate took his hand when my cousin hired him for his first acting job, the first movie I was ever in. But no one seemed more at home on a movie set than George. He understood the politics and alliances that emerge from these experiences, and as an intelligent student of movies, he learned how to navigate these situations with ease. And the second the opportunity presented itself to get to Hollywood, he jumped and never looked back.

We came out to Los Angeles at the same time, but George was smart in ways it took me longer to learn, and he was focused beyond reason. Sleeping in a friend's closet, schmoozing all the "gate keepers" and studio secretaries, whatever it took. He used his wit and connections and hard work to get him to the starting gate, and once heat was applied he took off. Again, preparation meets opportunity and *bang* - Oscar time, private jet time, paparazzi time. This was no accident, he just became more successful than anyone could've imagined. Go, George. I know he's a great guy to this day. That's hard to pull off.

Lou Diamond Phillips

As I stated earlier, I met Lou in Adam's class and this is where Lou came into his own as an actor. Never have I seen a more serious, focused approach to the work as Lou took. He was like a sponge, and with the immediate feedback of our playback sessions along with Adam's guidance, Lou flourished like no other actor I've since encountered.

He grew from being a rather theatrical actor into a much more subtle and powerful performer during that short time. There were so few opportunities for actors in Dallas then so there was little way forward for any of us, but Lou seemed destined for greatness. He became somewhat of a big shot on the local scene, picking up independent film work and writing his own scripts. It was as if he willed his way into the business.

After a couple of years, I ended up moving to L.A. around 1984 and started working pretty soon after. I came home to Dallas to visit after landing a couple of guest-starring roles on network TV. No one was happier for me than Lou, he acted as if it was a win for him also. It *was* a win for the Film Actors Lab in Arlington - one of their students was in Hollywood actually doing it. I think it was a real morale booster.

It wasn't long after that the producers of *La Bamba* went on a nationwide search for someone to play Richie Valens. This was unusual for a small indie film, but Lou ended up on the short list of viable actors for the role. He came out to L.A. and crashed on the couch of a woman he would later marry. Before you knew it, he was starring in his first Hollywood biopic that would forever change his destiny. It was not long before he was incredibly in demand. With *Stand and Deliver* and later the *Young Guns* franchise, he became a household name and the cool guy to have in your movie.

He's always the hardest working and best loved member of any cast or crew. And now as an emerging director, he's able to apply everything he's learned in front of the camera behind it. He's still the guy you want on your movie set, in either capacity.

What I can say about Lou is he's my flipping hero. He has been my longest standing friend in the business and has always tried to find a place for me in whatever he is directing. I've done several films for and with him. He's loyal to his friends and great to his fans. We continue to collaborate to this day.

Brad Pitt

Of all the folks I've mentioned here I spent the least amount of time with Brad, but what we did spend together gave me a good look at him before the world learned his name. Like George, he had an education and a good business head on his shoulders before he stepped across the state line. I know the most successful artists have the best business sense. When I worked with him, he had not been in Hollywood very long. He'd gotten off the bus from Missouri and dove in neck deep. He'd already had the infamous job as a chicken in front of El Pollo Loco but I was most interested in hearing about his days driving strippers to gigs all over town. I think it worked out pretty well for him.

It quickly became obvious that this guy had talent, and of course he looked exactly like a young Brad Pitt, so that didn't hurt. But mostly what he had, which seemed in abundance with my crowd, was a huge drive to succeed. And we were both pretty comfortable in our roles as hungry actors. That's its own motivation.

We freely fantasized about what it was going to be like when fame hit, which is why we started calling him Brad Turbo, because - come on? Who wants to see a movie starring a guy named "Brad Pitt"? Apparently a lot of people. Who knows how much living in a fantasy world of his own making had to do with his insane success, but in my mind, you can't separate the two.

I'm happy for him and his career is something to be extremely proud of. I knew once I saw *Thelma and Louise* his life would never be the same. And it wasn't. However, I wouldn't trade places with him for all his wealth and opportunity. He said it best himself in numerous interviews, that he wishes everyone could experience the fabulous life he's been handed because there's really no "there" there.

Brandon Lee

Here's the deal. Everything great seems inevitable in retrospect, but while it's going down, it's often a train wreck and far from a "sure thing." Brandon seemed destined for greatness from day one, but he actually had to become the avatar he'd chosen for himself long before he ever became great. He hadn't pursued martial arts or acting while in school but once out he knew he wanted to step into his father's shoes. Armed with the last name Lee (the most common last name on the planet), he'd have to become even better than his old man if he ever wanted respect. And he wanted respect. What he did have was his father's insane work ethic and ability to focus.

He enrolled in Emerson College in Boston for a short time but was soon getting offers to be in Chinese language martial arts films. Goodbye Emerson, Hello Hong Kong. Just before I met him he was in a TV movie called *Kung Fu, The Movie*. Now he could begin the journey that would end six years later on the set of *The Crow*.

The important thing is he understood he really wanted to do work that he could be proud of, it wasn't enough to just work. He understood the commercial aspect of action films and how that was likely his bread and butter, but eventually he was going to have a serious acting career or nothing at all.

Vendrell met him before Brandon filmed *KUNG FU: The Movie* and trained him for the audition. Brandon had not studied martial arts since his dad died, so he actually fell during his initial tryout doing a snap kick. So Mike had a weekend to get him ready for his next audition. Somehow they pulled it off and this was Brandon's start in becoming a world class martial artist in only a few years. By the time Brandon was at the end of his life at 28, he'd outshined his dad as a martial artist, according to those who knew or studied both. Brandon was one of the first to qualify as a Thai kickboxing instructor in the States. Pretty amazing stuff.

So having already done the leads in movies and TV shows, he decided to go get training. That's when Miggy suggested the Beverly Hills Playhouse. Brandon saw through the rules put there for no good reason, but he was paying to be there. We weren't in high school any longer but sometimes it felt like it, including ditching class and being highly disruptive. But what the hell, we had a million laughs and we were fully aware this was a temporary situation. Then came small theater productions with some very talented locals. Training, preparation, rehearsal, performance. Rinse and repeat, a thousand times. He got there. The transformation was a joy to see, and we both knew he was ready. His tenacity is what got him there, and the magic red carpet ride was about to begin. Boy, nothing was gonna stop him.

I was lucky enough to see his physical evolution as well. We were gym rats together and I still use the weightlifting program he and our friend, Daryl Chan, taught me. He was relentless in his pursuit of physical prowess, and he attacked it on several fronts.

Conditioning was the foundation of his professional life, so there was always running, lifting, swimming, boxing and a hundred other cardio activities. But his training didn't stop there. He was constantly in a martial arts class or training with his sensei, Mike Vendrell. Dan Inosanto, who was his father's training partner, still has an academy in Marina Del Rey that Brandon frequented, sometimes taking four classes in one night.

He prepared specifically for each movie, and his weight trainer, Darryl Chan, and I spent countless hours with him at Body Builders Gym in Silver Lake, helping him achieve whatever look he was going for. He was adamant on *The Crow* that he look almost skeletal, think Mick Jagger thin. For him that meant dropping about 20 lbs. of muscle. He kept himself to 1500 calories a day while spending six hours a day at the gym. It sounds crazy as I write this, but that's what he did.

I became aware that he studied his father's career and life more than anyone. His dad offered a template for success, there for the bold to follow. And Brandon was nothing if not bold. He saw what his father set out to do and how to achieve the desired result and was well on his way.

Bruce had to figure out how become an icon on

his own and he was very open about how he did it. Now all anyone has to do is follow his prescription. For my generation, Bruce was as big a deal as a Beatle. We were all beating the crap out of each other with home-made nunchucks made out of broomsticks.

In death, Bruce has emerged as something more than a fallen movie star, the streets of Tinsel Town are choked with those. Bruce has become a modern Confucius, a person who lived the wisdom that he shared with the world. And for those of us who were alive during his lifetime, most will never be the same. I can think of no other actor who achieved that kind of status.

However, Brandon was on track to eclipse all that came before him. With multiple picture deals with multiple major studios, folks were lining up to make him rich and successful beyond measure. And with his vision and focus, he was ready to knock the world off its axis. What a loss...

I'm quite sure, had he known how it would end, he'd have lived his life in the same way. He was aware that reality is just smoke and mirrors, but this was *his* playground and he would not be denied his joy. His career happened because preparation met opportunity. Celebrity for him was just beginning, and the lives he touched will forever feel his loss.

FAN Q & A

Q: M.D. asks, *"What was the biggest challenge, as an actor, to give the believability that you were immersed in the BMX world?"*

A: "Keeping my feet on the pedals during takes, and not being caught dating the stunt riders' girlfriends. It was my duty as an actor to see what it would be like to date a girl who sleeps with actual BMXers. Anything for my art. You're welcome."

Q: W.F. asks, *"What was it like to work with Rocky's wife and My Favorite Martian?"*

A: "It was like working with Don Corleone's daughter, and the judge on *Picket Fences*."

Q: C.S. asks, *"How rad was it to do love scenes with Lori Loughlin?"*

A: "Crazy rad. And the fact that it was recorded on film! I'll always be that guy who made out with a 23-year-old Lori Loughlin. Although my wife would tell me she's hotter. And I have to agree. (*No really, I have to - she made me.*)"

Q: G.B. asks, *"What was it like to work with one of the greatest stuntmen of all time, Hal Needham?"*

A: "I take offense at the designation of Hal as 'one' of the greatest stuntmen of all time. His record demands the title of THE greatest stuntman that will ever be, unless Satan unleashes some sort of freaking UBER-demon that plans to use movie stunts to rule the world. Hal was the nicest, humblest, and most colorful man one can meet. For being the toughest hombre in any room he walked into for his whole life, his humility was rare indeed. And with a newly-minted Oscar on his widow's mantle, he continues to inspire and speak to a whole new generation of moviemakers and goers. Bringing *RAD* to the world and his innovations included in the film are only a small part of his staggering resume. We won't likely be able to truly appreciate his contribution to the film industry for years. His direction to me was minimal, aside from telling me how his buddy Burt would've done it, something I really appreciated at the time, being a young actor with little to hang onto."

Q: M.T. asks, *"Did you have to wear special underwear when filming the 'ass sliding' scene with Lori?"*

A: "Nothing special. My typical Kevlar-lined, bullet and bomb proofed undies, with an extra, EXTRA large cup."

Q: JP asks, *"How was it kissing Lori in that skintight Mongoose outfit, without getting a chubby?"*

A: "Thanks to my Kevlar cup, she was safe from any embarrassing moments, until the cup exploded, injuring four crew members but fortunately giving me several new holes to pee through."

My RAD Career

Q: E.S. asks, *"Why does RAD continue to have such an enduring place in the hearts of its fans?"*

A: "Most likely what you are experiencing is heart worm or some other type of parasite. Consult your physician immediately. Or it's the fact that the top action director of the day had the writers craft a script that would best display the talents of the world-class athletes that invented the sport, and thereby introduced BMX to millions who looked at it as a key element in the development of their psyche. But I think it's the heart worm."

Q: B.L. asks, *"Did you perform any of Cru's stunts in the movie? If so, which ones?"*

A: "I detailed in this book that my biggest stunt was not going to the premiere of the movie. As far as my career was concerned, I might as well have given Mother Theresa crabs."

Q: M.B. asks, *"Who hooked up with who on the set?"*

A: "My lawyer told me not to divulge such personal information. It was... *THE TWINS*. You know, with each other."

Q: T.P. asks, *"Did he really say, 'The porch, I've told you a thousand times, THE PORCH,' a thousand times?"*

A: "If you were here right now, I'd beat the crap out of you."

Q: E.S. asks, *"How was it being around all those great old school BMXers, and what was the scene like?"*

A: "At the time they were new school BMXers and they had not grown into the calloused a-holes they have become. Sad really. Still, it doesn't sully the memory of the glue huffing thieves that spent their off hours 'borrowing' bikes from the local elementary schools. Other than that, a greater group of guys you'll be hard-pressed to find."

Q: L.E. asks, *"Was there ever talk of RAD II and would you have taken on the role of Cru Jones again?"*

A: "After two decades of babbling, '*RAD II, RAD II,*' incessantly, my shrink wondered if there was any talk BESIDES *RAD II*. And since my entire adult life since *RAD* has been an unfortunate attempt at recapturing those glory days, my unrelenting quest for fame has demanded I offer myself at parties as a living Cru Jones mannequin. For free. So, yeah, I might consider it."

Q: F.B. asks, *"Why did we not see the movie in France, so I would have spared hours of translation?"*

A: "I specifically asked producers to NOT release it in France - I'm still a bit miffed at that WWII thing."

Q: T.P. asks, *"Did you ever take those SATs?"*

A: "Did you ever get a life?"

Q: S.M. asks, *"Did you have any idea that you were taking part and contributing to such a huge chapter in BMX and freestyle worldwide? RAD spawned thousands of new BMX fanatics worldwide."*

A: "I was hoping to be added to Mount Rushmore, but worldwide adoration doesn't suck. I'm actually so proud to be a part of something that meant so much to so many. To add to the legacy is something I'm now fully committed to, solely due to fan support."

Q: D.H. asks, *"Did you ever learn any BMX tricks?"*

A: "Yes, the three most important words in their vocabulary, 'Deny, deny, deny.'"

Q: D.H. asks, *"Did you even like BMX, or was it just a role?"*

A: "I was unaware of the sport when I got the part, but I never treat my jobs as 'just another role.' I was extremely excited to have the lead in a major film that I thought would move the ball forward. However, no one could have anticipated The X Games, The Olympics, and the tricks that are being pulled off that are now considered routine."

Q: J.M. asks, *"If you could ride for any BMX factory team now, which one would it be?"*

A: "Does *Playboy* sponsor BMX teams?"

Q: J.K. asks, *"When did you realize what an impact your character had on extreme sports and The Olympics?"*

A: "I'm not sure of a particular instance, but after hearing from literally thousands of fans and being referred to by countless TV shows and movies (anyone catch *Hot Rod* starring Andy Samberg?), it's something that will clearly outlive the people who made the film (hopefully not me)."

Q: S.L. asks, *"What happened to the Corvette and all that cash?"*
A: "Christian loaded the trunk with the dough, and took off with Becky (yes, Becky!) *Thelma and Louise* style. They were last seen at a regional BMX race, filling the tires of bikes without an air pump."

Q: M.S. asks, *"What if Cru raced BMX and was a Kung Fu master, and fought BMX Ninjas - what then?"*
A: "You are obviously an astute observer and have vast insight into what makes Cru tick. I have alerted the authorities, you psycho, so put on your tinfoil hat, and wait for the nice officers outside."

Q: D.M. asks, *"Did you have any idea that after 30 years, people would still be talking about this movie?"*
A: "Prognosticating what would happen decades from then, I only envisioned Twitter and Facebook, and unfortunately somebody stole my best ideas. :(My prediction for three decades from now includes a mortician stuffing my ass full of cotton. Thank you."

Q: A.L. asks, *"Was Cru's Mum married to Rocky Balboa before or after the movie, and if before, does that mean that Rocky is Cru's dad?"*
A: "You have noticed the freakish resemblance between our bodies, so have found me out. We are nearly identical in every way, apart from his shrunken balls. I have decided Stallone is aware of his paternity obligations, hence the ignoring of my phone calls and countless texts."

Q: E.G. asks, *"Do you find strangers come up and ask if you're Cru Jones more than they ask if you're Bill Allen?"*

A: "I occasionally get recognized as Cru, however the only people who ask if I'm Bill Allen tend to be UPS men and summons servers. My favorite story of being recognized in public deserves a retelling...

"One time I was visiting my parents in Dallas, and Brandon was with me. We went to the local public swimming pool to stave off the ungodly heat, and some kid came up and asked me my name. I replied 'Bill Allen,' and the poor little guy started shaking and repeating, 'I knew it!' He then asked Brandon if he was in *RAD* and deflated when Brandon said he was just my manservant. One of the mothers found out we were actors, and asked Brandon what we were doing at a public swimming pool. Brandon replied that we were getting our portraits put on the bottom of our private pool in mosaics. He was good."

Q: M.R. asks, *"Did you get a chub ass sliding with Lori Loughlin?"*

A: "Dude, I'd 'get a chub' if YOU went ass sliding with Lori."

Q: A.A. asks, *"Whatever happened to all them BMX bikes? Most was broke of course, would they be in a movie/and maybe even updated? Who will be the replacement riders???"*

A: "I only published this letter to show the sad state of our educational system."

Q: J.B. asks, *"How much did you actually ride during filming, and what were your thoughts/expectations when you got the role of Cru Jones?"*

A: "I was riding a lot on that iconic bike (wish I had it now) and spent as much time as I could to look natural just riding it. The doubles they had for me left me no need to learn any real tricks. There are a couple of times you see me nearly lose it in the film - one is when I crash through the fence with Hell Track painted on it. It was convenient that they had hinges placed high up so I could go through it, nonetheless you can see me nearly come off that bike. The other time is when I qualify during the preliminary race, just before the confrontation scene with Talia. I put on my front brakes first and fly into the crowd of my friends waiting for me. Again, it was a happy accident that made the shot much more dynamic."

Q: A.R. asks, *"How does it feel to be an icon?"*

A: "Largely undeserved. Can I borrow five bucks?"

Q: S.R. asks, *"Can you sign my boobs?"*

A: [*I granted the request later. He had a great rack, by the way.*]

Q: J.F. asks, *"I want to know where I can go ass sliding?"*

A: "Ass sliding is a place in your mind, much like OZ, but so cold, parts will freeze off."

Q: J.F. asks, *"Do you regret opening up this discussion/questions to everyone?"*

A: "I regret the discovery of fire, the rest is just details."

Q: J.C. asks, *"Dear Bill, how come there has never been a sequel? Will there ever be a sequel, and will you reprise the role or be involved in it any other way?"*

A: "There have been numerous attempts to make a sequel and/or a remake for decades, but there is still hope. Keep up the *RAD* talk. I'm committed to bringing the fans something for their support, so stay tuned."

Q: A.R. asks, *"Hey Bill, I rode for Mat Hoffman in the '90s, and he has become an icon over the years, just like you. Do you actually feel BMX is a part of you, or was it a role, and not what you truly did like Mat?"*

A: "To be spoken about in the same breath as Mat is something I really don't deserve, nor do I take lightly. To achieve fame in the BMX arena, Mat not only risked his life for the sport, HE LITERALLY DIED FOR THE SPORT. Sure, he came back from the dead after flatlining, *LIKE JESUS*, but that did not stop him from participating and continuing to innovate. All I did was have the time of my life for six weeks in Canada, just for showing up on time. My worst sport injury came from eating bad chicken at a softball game. Not to mention Mat literally kept the sport alive in the '90s when it had fallen from public favor. So being compared to a man for whom there is no comparison is mind-blowing."

Q: B.K. asks, *"Cru, besides landing the backflip at Hell Track, what is the best trick you ever landed?"*

A: "I once landed in jail after getting my ID stolen, because the guy who stole it had opened a Blockbuster account and never returned $500 worth of video games. (Yup – grand theft... If not for a handwriting analyst, I could still be rotting there now!) A warrant was put out for my arrest, and I spent a night in a West Hollywood holding tank, and somehow got out of there still a 'mouth virgin.' Best trick ever."

Q: P.B. asks, *"How does it feel that you have inspired tens of thousands of kids to ride freestyle bikes?"*

A: "I feel wildly under compensated for sending a generation of kids to the ER. Mike Tyson went through several fortunes hurting people. Me? Nuthin'."

Q: A.S, asks, *"What was your favorite piece of fan made art?"*

A:

Q: J.V. asks, *"What was it like pashing with Lori Loughlin?!?!?!?!?! She's hot!!"*

A: 'Pashing' is synonymous with French kissing (which I call 'freedom kissing') which Wikipedia defines as, 'A kiss in which one or both participants' tongues touch the partner's lips or tongue, usually entering their mouth. A French kiss is a slow, passionate kiss which is usually considered intimate, romantic, erotic or sexual.' I just wanted to clear that up. That's what I did with Lori. As for what it was like, you be the judge."

Q: J.H. asks, *"If they made a sequel today, would you even be interested? Like now Cru is a shop or* *company owner. Or maybe he left the scene and dropped out for decades, riding flatland in a little parking garage at night and is brought back into the scene by a young rider trying to make it. Where would you see the role of Cru Jones continuing in today's world?"*

A: "Obviously J.H. (if that is your real name), on top of being an amateur BMX rider, you are clearly an amateur hacker cyber-freak who has stolen my original idea for the sequel. YOU HAVE DISCLOSED OFFICIAL SHOW BUSINESS INTELLECTUAL PROPERTY AND WILL BE PROSECUTED TO THE FULL EXTENT OF SHOW BUSINESS LAW. I demand you send me your complete email history, along with any notes or alternate endings you'd think might help the story along. You might be eligible for a 'Stolen By' credit on the movie. Bend over and grab your ankles - the showbiz cops are on their way."

Q: C.T. asks, *"Was that you doing backflips onto the mattress, or was that a stuntman?"*

A: "For those who don't have time to read the whole book and just skipped to this Q&A section, it was absolutely me, doing pretty much every stunt. Yeah, that's it. I did 'em all."

Q: S.T. asks, *"What was it like to work with Bart Conner?"*

A: "It was like a Greek God coming down from Mount Olympus and showing the rest of us exactly how inadequate we are. It was as if purple lightning bolts came out of his butt and burned us mere mortals to a crisp with the sheer power of his awesomeness. Aside from that, he was pretty cool."

Q: C.S. asks, *"What was it like witnessing history and being a part of the backflip?"*

A: "My only part was looking cool when I pretended to land the trick. And, therefore, a generation of kids grew up thinking I did it, when Jose was the one who pulled it off. But I TOLD him to do it, so I pretty much rule."

Q: T.S. asks, *"Do you still go ass sliding? That looked like so much fun."*

A: "To answer that would turn an R-rated book to an X. My main hobby is desperation, and when that gets old, it's powered parachuting. If you wanna learn how to fly powered parachutes, go to www.paraplane.com. Call Phil. He's a lot like the drill instructor from *Full Metal Jacket*, but he'll keep you alive."

Q: B.G. asks, *"What was your favorite song from the soundtrack?"*

A: "Fans might find this shocking, but the whole soundtrack is pretty much like nails on a chalkboard to me. I'm more of a Beatles/Stones guy, so I never could understand the big hair and synthesizer generation. I'm sure John Farnham is a nice guy and all, but if I was stuck on a deserted island with only that soundtrack, I would swim back to civilization just to kill him, and then swim back to the island."

Q: S.P. asks, *"Did you ever imagine Mat Hoffman and 100 other old school legends would watch the movie at the old school reunion?"*

A: "My imagination never has me picturing a bunch of old smelly guys sitting around. It usually has me thinking of a scenario involving Pam Anderson, mayonnaise and sand, but thanks for asking."

Q: B.R. asks, *"I want to know which stuntman lived on Corey Lane in West Hills? Me and a group of kids were riding around and this guy rolls up and started doing tricks and showed us his garage full of freestyle bikes, he said he was a stuntman from the movie RAD, said he was the guy on top of the semi during the parade. I asked Eddie, but he said it wasn't him. Anyway, that was my question."*

A: "I kind of zoned out while reading your question, but if it was, 'Am I planning to kill myself after reading it?' the answer is a resounding yes."

Q: S.E. (Who's a dude by the way) asks, *"To Cru, can I have this bicycle dance with you? But with this song. Plug in your fave now..."*

A: "WTF???!!!"

Q: P.M. asks, *"Do you own any memorabilia from the movie?"*

A: "Yes, a cold sore from Miss Teen Calgary, but I can't get anything for it on EBAY."

Q: T.K. asks, *"I grew up dreaming I could be as good as Cru Jones, and I'm sure I'm not the only* *guy that felt that way. How does it feel to have such a positive effect on fans of the movie?"*

A: "Like a pebble thrown in a pond, the ripple effect is wide ranging and extremely gratifying. As this book has shown I have often used poor judgment and although *RAD* does not mitigate that fact, it allows me to feel that I've had a part in something that has inspired so many, and maybe that might offer some sort of boon in my next life. Or I might come back as the lowest form of life yet discovered - a Hollywood agent."

Bill Allen

ACKNOWLEDGEMENTS

Big thanks to: Carol Allen, Linda Sivertsen, Sherman Allen, David Fagan, Jill Fagan, Tony Donaldson, Jeremy Moser, Daniel Tosh, Aimee Springer, and Bobby Collins and the great team at Beacon Publishing Group.

Mostly I want to thank *RAD* fans and the BMX community, and anyone who has ever bought this book.

ABOUT THE AUTHOR

Photo and cover photo by Tony Donaldson

Bill Allen is an actor/musician living in Los Angeles with his wife, his angry dog, and too many cats. Visit www.billallenrad.net, www.myradcareer.com and www.themovierad.com

www.ingramcontent.com/pod-product-compliance
Lightning Source LLC
Chambersburg PA
CBHW030321100526
44592CB00010B/521